5·15·78

Decent Housing: A Promise to Keep

Decent Housing:
A Promise to Keep

Federal Housing Policy
and its Impact on the City

An account of how the
federal government has
attempted to help the cities
get rid of their slums; the promises
kept and broken, the progress
real and illusory, and an
assessment of future prospects.

Tom Forrester Lord

SCHENKMAN PUBLISHING COMPANY, INC.
Cambridge, Massachusetts
02138

Copyright © 1977
Schenkman Publishing Company, Inc.
3 Mt. Auburn Place
Cambridge, Massachusetts 02138

Library of Congress Cataloging in Publication Data

Lord, Tom Forrester.
    Decent housing.

    1. Housing policy—United States.   I.   Title.
HD7293.L65   301.5'4'0973   76-26714
ISBN 0-87073-491-1

Printed in the United States of America

To Stacey, Clark, and Forrester, my children

For what are all our contrivings,
And the wisdom of our books,
When compared with your caresses,
And the gladness of your looks?

Longfellow

CONTENTS

ACKNOWLEDGMENTS

Except for the fortunate opportunity to lecture at Rice University and do research while on the staff of the University of Houston's Institute for Urban Studies, I could not have found the tranquillity and time to write this book. So I am grateful for the invitation extended to me first by Jack Mitchell and then by David Crane, Director and Dean of the Architecture Department at Rice.

To Ralph Conant, formerly Director of the Institute for Urban Studies and now President of Shimer College, I am deeply indebted. In spite of his many projects related to urban scholarship, he took the time to read and, at several stages, make changes in the manuscript, always improving it. Mostly, though, I appreciate his inspiration and confidence—he is at once scholar, teacher, and thoughtful citizen. His encouragement of a practitioner to take up the pen is greatly appreciated.

When I think of what the book is about—an attempt to portray the successes and failures of federal housing policy in the cities —I am immediately constrained to acknowledge the gratitude I feel to all those fellow soldiers in the struggle to improve housing. First, my colleagues in the Houston Housing Development and Management Corporations have helped provide a perspective on both the strengths and weaknesses of urban housing programs. Second, I want to acknowledge publicly an appreciation I often express privately to Jackson C. Hinds and George L. McGonigle, two business leaders who have given so generously of their best efforts to make the opportunity for a better home open to all. What I have achieved I owe to them, and when I have failed they have been there to give me stamina to press on.

Third, I thank the two men who first shaped my career, Julius Allen at the Library of Congress, and James Twomey at Urban America. They gambled on a novice, and if nothing else, I am now a veteran!

Others who deserve a special thanks for reading the manuscript are James King, Terry Lord, Clovis Heimsath, Lynn Cooksey, John Mixon and Bernard Frieden. I thank them for the errors they caught and the insights they gave. For the hints I did not take from them, I apologize.

Linda Carman transcribed scratchy tapes of lectures which formed the beginnings of *Decent Housing: A Promise To Keep*. She also was a participant in some of the events described and helped me write about them so others could see what we saw. Wanda Anderson typed the later drafts, with patience and competence.

It has also been a pleasure to have the good humor and wise guidance of Alfred Schenkman on this voyage into print.

And, finally, a word of appreciation to my wife Katharine for her steady enthusiasm and patience.

June 1, 1976
Houston, Texas

PREFACE

America, in its post-Watergate and post-Vietnam phase, desperately seeks a chastened optimism. All of us want a restored confidence in ourselves as a people and a new measure of trust in our leaders.

The wish for a retreat from the turmoil caused by an ill-fated war adventure and a near fatal attack on our institutions by a misguided President and his minions is not sufficient to stem the tide of mounting challenges facing America in the mid-1970's.

While we desire a pause from (deserved) criticism of recent political events, the onrush of problems to face will not be quelled.

The crime rate rises almost uncontrollably. Unemployment hovers at rates higher than any since the Depression, and ominously, many have come to accept these rates of joblessness as normal. Fuel price rises have tangibly diminished the quality of life for millions—with more devastating effects yet to come.

In this context I would have preferred to write an "upbeat" book —one that would contribute to equanimity and even some joy. I am not comfortable as nay-sayer and purveyor of ill tidings.

But as with crime, unemployment, and energy, the picture I see for decent housing in America is not bright. And so I am constrained to describe what is.

Unless the course we are on with respect to housing policy in the United States is radically altered, the ordinary dream of every American for adequate shelter will be as obsolete as a 25¢ gallon of gasoline.

Housing policy is primarily determined by Washington officials, in the White House, the Office of Management and Budget, the Department of Housing and Urban Development, and by Congress. General economic conditions as well as federal fiscal and monetary policies have an enormous impact on the production of housing, but the real determinant of whether the American people shall be decently housed is the strength of the federal incentives and programs by government.

That is why this book focuses on the housing policies and programs in Washington over the last forty years. Housing is a "political" subject. So we deal with the convergencies and confluences of interests, personalities, issues, and historical events which have carried us to the present housing conditions confronting the American people.

xi

Why should Americans listen to a Houstonian on this subject? The nation's perspective of Space City USA is not likely to square with one of its citizens proposing to write about national urban problems and how they have been attacked, successfully or unsuccessfully. Most Americans seem to believe Houston is so unlike the other large cities that it cannot serve as any comparison. Recently, the Mayor of Detroit, Coleman Young, came away from the U. S. Conference of Mayors in Boston with this opinion:

> "The City of Houston . . . is in another world. Obviously Houston is not a prototype for large cities. Houston feasts on the carcasses of the rest of us because it is an oil center. Houston's problems differ from those of New York and Chicago."[1]

The first response of most of us in Houston is probably a certain smug, "Yes, and aren't we lucky." To some extent, it is true. Unemployment is one-half of the national average; growth and prosperity are facts of life in Houston.

Yet another response contains some faint exasperation—like that which comes when all Texans are pictured as rich oil men or gun-toting cowboys. Houston is fortunate, yes, but even here nearly 100,000 families are living in substandard structures or paying too much for their housing.

Also Houston has, over the last ten years, tried to give attention to these problems. From a deep cultural antipathy to participation in any federal program—looked on as poisonous socialism—the present Mayor, Fred Hofheinz, and his predecessor, Louie Welch, have brought the city cautiously, but effectively, toward matching the benefits of federal urban programs to the needs of its less fortunate citizens.

Houston's problems and its attempts at solutions are not substantially different from those of other cities elsewhere.

Thus I hope the following pages, with their effort to reveal where our cities have been and where they are going in regard to housing policy, will be of interest to concerned citizens throughout the land. The effort will be rewarded if housing policy makers in Washington make a positive commitment to keep the promise of a decent home for all Americans.

Men who live in hovels are not citizens.
They are abandoned to bad food and bad skin,
bad teeth, bad shortages, filth, rags, and roaches,
all the states of rage, failure, and classic shame.

from "Hovel"
by
Bink Noll

INTRODUCTION: HOUSING
IN THE PUBLIC ARENA

The purpose of this essay is to bring historical perspective and contemporary analysis to the shaping of American housing policy in the public arena—an arena in which the individual citizen as housing consumer is the primary participant. Housing consumers are too diverse and unorganized to speak with one voice; therefore, it has fallen to the nation's elected representatives to commit to the written word, in the form of legislation, what they suppose to be the will of consumers. Those representatives are usually acting on the more unified and explicit expressions of those men and groups more directly involved in the housing industry: builders, lenders, investors, suppliers, tradesmen, managers, brokers; in short, those whose livelihood depends on the continual output of housing for the American people.

Out of the press of "special" interests competing for those benefits, together with congressmen responding to the will of their constituents, comes housing legislation. For better or worse, this is the way it has been and will be unless we transform our present democratic system.

The person, therefore, who desires to understand our housing policy and to influence its direction would do well to observe the public arena in which the hopes of the ill-housed, the interests of the industry, and the political talents of the public official converge and do their alchemy on our national housing legislation.

The Housing Process in America

Housing is complex; it involves design, construction, and management. It also has a financial aspect; the country is run on the basis of private investment, so Wall Street is interested in housing. There is also the legislative and governmental side.

Financially, there are areas of cooperation and agreement among all these sectors. At one level, the individual consumer expresses his need for housing via his visit to the savings and loan or mortgage company, or to a landlord. This sets off a reaction that goes to the heart of all the other areas. He creates an area of agreement; the businessman will supply his need in order to earn his livelihood. The man on Wall Street wants to have a good market in which to place his investments. The housing market can only be good as long as people are expressing their need.

3

The government, too, has an interest because it responds to the other three sectors. It responds to the investor, the consumer, and the industry. The consumer, either consciously or unconsciously, wants or needs the government to help him when the landlord sets the rent at a figure above his ability to pay.

The government at the local level enforces the housing code so that the house remains standard, and thereby protects the consumer's health and safety.

These are areas of interest. Seldom do all of the interests meet in areas of cooperation. In fact, the only times they really do meet are in times of economic distress, for example, in the 1930's. When Leon Keyserling and others had drafted the Housing Act of 1937, Senator Wagner called up to the White House to get an appointment to discuss the program with President Roosevelt. After some political discussion, the President asked Keyserling, "By the way, Leon, who is going to sell the bricks?" In other words, who is really going to benefit, and conversely, who is going to be left out. Those are the key questions to ask about a housing program. Times of economic distress such as the 30's, when all the forces met, created far-reaching, groundbreaking legislation. In the democratic lingo, something was beneficial to everyone. The consumer got the housing promised and delivered. The industry got jobs, and therefore earnings and profits. The Wall Street community got a new market.

In 1968, another convergence of interests occurred, resulting in the passage of the Housing and Urban Development Act of 1968. After the Housing Act of 1968 and the Tax Reform Act of 1969 had passed, limited partnerships in subsidized housing were very hot on Wall Street. Even the large brokerage firms began to syndicate housing partnerships. In fact, a National Corporation for Housing Partnerships was formed by the Congress and made part of the Act of 1968. Under it, the President formed the board of a public corporation which went to the private sector for stock subscriptions. All were to be in denominations of not less than $100,000. Investment was made at the local level in housing and in syndicating housing partnerships. There was a tremendous interest on the part of the investment group in housing. It was less than in 1937, however, when there was public financing. The Public Housing Act passed in 1937 created a tremendous new enterprise for the Wall Street bond market and the bond houses who sold bonds to finance a million units of housing.

In 1937 and in 1968, when a politician asked, "Who sells the

4

bricks?" he got a positive answer, in that some of his friends or constituents in the brick business would benefit, as well as his supporters in a wide range of building enterprises.

Under normal conditions of economic stability, however, the housing coalition falls apart. In times of prosperity, the money markets on Wall Street are attracted to interests other than housing, such as equity markets, corporate bonds, and commercial loans. We can define economic prosperity as a time of full employment, high productivity, and high industrial output. The steel mills operating at full capacity are a good indicator. In the face of these competitive capital markets, housing suffers and becomes less attractive to investors.

The consumer's ability to borrow money decreases. Times of prosperity have a negative effect on the poor if the housing industry is considered. Builders focus their attention normally on upper income housing because it is more profitable. In 1950, it would have been much more profitable to build a $20,000 house than two $10,000 houses. Today it is much more profitable to build an $80,000 house than four $20,000 houses. It takes less time to build an $80,000 house than four $20,000 houses. Also, when the house is completed, it is easier to find a qualified buyer of an $80,000 house, because someone interested in the $80,000 house will not have any problems with finance. The persons wanting to buy $20,000 houses may have problems at the credit bureau. They are not necessarily insurmountable, but there are problems. The builders, who have all the jobs they can do, know that. The best example of this occurred in 1971 and 1972. In those years, 2 million and 2.6 million new houses were built respectively. Nearly 25 percent of all those starts involved subsidized units. Because of the phenomenon of appealing to the upper income market during prosperous years, nothing would have been built for the poor unless the government had had a subsidized program. That was the incentive to build for the people needing subsidy.

During prosperity, disharmony among the four elements of the housing enterprise is normal.

Housing tends to decline, at least relatively, when the economy as a whole booms. The reason is that the mortgage market is at a disadvantage in a thriving financial market. In periods of growth, high-yield stocks and bonds are more attractive to investors than mortgages on the secondary market.

The secondary market is the means of keeping a supply of funds available to primary lending institutions. If investors do not buy up lenders' home mortgages, funds are not available for further loans to home buyers. In such a situation, the pressure to increase interest rates on the primary mortgage mounts. But higher interest rates only make the individual home buyer more reluctant to purchase a new home. This "tight money" situation depresses the housing industry as a whole—even though the total economy is growing.

To illustrate this relationship of the housing industry to the total economy, we may observe the period from 1954 to mid-1957 and the period from late 1965 to the present.

Housing starts experienced a downward trend after 1955, a trend which was slightly reversed in 1958. The total economy, however, was experiencing inflationary pressures during 1956 and 1957. In 1955 prices were stable; in 1956 and 1957 the price index rose significantly (increasing by 3 percent during 1956 and 2.9 percent in 1957). During this period, the Federal Reserve Board sought to combat inflation by seven successive raises in the discount rate. The average yield on long-term United States Government bonds and notes went up to a high of 3.6 percent in 1956 from 2.5 percent in August 1954. Other types of securities naturally rose correspondingly. As a result, many investors shifted out of the mortgage market into these areas where returns were more attractive, with the result that there was a drop in the number of housing starts.

In late 1965 and 1966 a precipitous drop occurred in housing starts. For instance, in September 1965 there were 124.300 nonfarm housing starts; in September 1966 there were 92,800.

Again, it is possible to relate this drop in the housing market to federal monetary policy. On December 5, 1965, the Federal Reserve Board raised the discount rate from 4 to 4½ percent. The Board also increased the interest rate allowable on certificates of deposit in commercial banks. These actions had wide ramifications in the money market, driving rates up and increasing yields on government securities. This tightening of money, combined with intense commercial and industrial demand for funds, severely limited the money available for mortgage lending. As before, with higher yields on other investments, investors generally avoided the secondary money market and took money from mortgage lending institutions, primarily savings and loan associations. Furthermore, business, with rising profits and demand, drained funds from other institutions such as commercial banks, funds which might otherwise have been used for mortgage loans.

Thus, the dip in housing starts is closely related to decreased savings. For example, in the summer of 1974 the annual rate of housing starts dropped 50 percent below the national goal of 2.6 million units, down from 2.152 million in July 1973. In August 1974 $1.6 billion was withdrawn from federally insured savings and loan associations.

Over the past thirty years, the federal government has become more involved not only in the sense of having programs that subsidize people, but in terms of the influence on finance. The Federal Reserve policy is by far the most influential factor on housing in this country. The Federal Reserve Board sets the discount rate, which in turn determines what the consumer will pay for loans.

The second most influential factor is the money supply, also controlled by the Federal Reserve. Housing is always at the mercy of federal monetary policy. The Federal Reserve Board, which sees itself as the defender of the country against inflation, uses its great powers to set the discount rate and to determine the supply of money. Its first victim is usually housing.

There is a close correspondence among Wall Street, the housing industry, and the government. Because their livelihoods are so dependent upon government policy, and not just the housing subsidy programs which they have supported, the National Association of Home Builders is almost required to have the strongest lobby in Washington. The President of the National Association of Home Builders is a regular visitor to Mr. Arthur Burns at the Federal Reserve Board to try to obtain policies with a more positive impact on housing. (In 1975 the President of the NAHB was J. S. Norman, Jr. of Houston. He recently related that at the Annual Banquet of NAHB Directors, Chairman and Mrs. Burns asked why there was such a wonderful orchestra playing while no one was dancing. Mr. Norman promptly asked Mrs. Burns to dance. The Chairman then asked Mrs. Norman and so the two couples had a delightful dance before the Chairman took his leave. I am sure Mr. Norman wishes his professional relations with the Federal Reserve Board Chairman were always as harmonious!)

The role and influence of the consumer on housing policy is a very broad subject that concerns the essence of democracy. A strong argument has been made that the real reason for the passage of the 1968 Housing Act was the turmoil in the cities, especially in the spring of 1968, when Martin Luther King, Jr. was killed. That year, the streets of Washington were aflame. Lyndon Johnson, as an American Democratic politician, responded to the ghetto problems and to the demands of the civil rights leaders that the cities had to be rebuilt. That was one answer to the problems of the ghetto.

The consumers, the people who benefit from the programs enacted by Congress, have some power. When their voice is spoken and heard, we have some kind of housing policy. Probably one of the reasons that housing is depressed today is because of the blunting of the civil rights movement.

People who believe that the subsidized housing programs failed can find allies among the poor. There are people living in public housing or in subsidized housing who agree that the programs were a failure. Obviously, tenants in public housing projects which are plagued by robbers and drug addicts express rejection of their environment and sometimes blame the housing officials or the public housing program for their plight. Of course, concentrating hundreds of poor, mostly fatherless, families into one housing project, no matter what its physical condition, is destined to favor a high incidence of criminality. So the public housing itself is not necessarily to blame. On the other hand, it is sometimes the case that poor management and a hostile bureaucracy can engender negative tenant attitudes, and when this occurs the public housing authority and its program are justly criticized.

From my own experience in managing subsidized housing, I have seen that the best constructed and managed project cannot forestall violent and destrictive behavior by those few persons who have never known any other kind of life. Therefore, even in the best housing developments for lower-income families there will always be conflict between management and the violence-prone who must be evicted in order to protect the welfare and safety of the other tenants who want peace and harmony. Thus the consumer can have a negative influence as well as a positive one.

The point of all this is that we get the kind of programs we do when the consumer, the industry, the investor, and the government reach a consensus as to what is needed. When one or more of the parties leaves the alliance, it falls apart. In January 1973 the Nixon Administration placed a moratorium on all subsidized housing programs, walking away from an agreement about housing. By and large the industry and the investment community supported the programs and are still arguing that they should be reinstated. But a concert of interest in housing has still to wait for a slowing of the inflationary spiral so that capital will be available for construction, as well as a new commitment by Federal officials to a revived housing industry.

I. AN HISTORICAL SKETCH OF FEDERAL HOUSING LEGISLATION, 1934-1974

National concern about poor housing conditions was sporadic until the 1930's, even though the slums of New York City teemed with new immigrants in the 19th century. A survey by a citizens association in 1864 inspired the adoption of the first tenement house law three years later. The United States Congress ordered a special investigation of urban blight in 1892, prompted in part by Jacob Riis' graphic description of slum conditions in *How the Other Half Lives*, published in 1890.

No substantial efforts beyond local enactment of codes resulted from such studies. A national response had to await the New Deal, an era when President Franklin D. Roosevelt declared that one-third of the nation was "ill-housed, ill-clothed, and ill-nourished." In the depths of the Depression, when foreclosures were wiping out homeowners at the rate of a thousand a day and driving them into the slums, the nation awoke at last and heard the cries from the tenement wilderness.

To stem the foreclosure tide, the federal government put liquid funds into the hands of lending institutions and provided insurance on new mortgages. These measures were accomplished by the National Housing Act of 1934, the law which created the Federal Housing Administration. The homes of America's middle class were saved, and a new pattern of mortgage financing was begun, based on the new concept of the long-term loan with a low down payment. It is the factor most responsible for America's home-ownership rate of 63 percent.

However, much more was needed if the housing needs of the poor were to be met. Harold Ickes had launched a housing construction program as a part of the Public Works Administration. The federal government built nearly twenty-five thousand homes in various localities in 1934-35, until a Federal Court of Appeals, ruling on a case arising in Louisville, Kentucky, declared the procedure unconstitutional. In order not to endanger the whole PWA program, the government did not appeal to the Supreme Court. Rather, a new approach was designed by housing officials and sponsored by Senator Robert Wagner of New York. The United States Housing Act of 1937 provided for the creation of local public housing authorities, which were authorized to sell bonds backed by the U. S. Government, to finance the development of housing for low-income

9

families. In addition, the federal government promised to pay an annual subsidy to retire the debt. It was expected that tenant rents would cover operating expenses:

Congress justified its passage of the Act on three grounds: 1) It would eliminate slums, 2) It would provide adequate housing for low-income families, and 3) It would alleviate unemployment.

The Act was barely passed and being implemented when World War II put a halt to construction. But, the wartime migrations to the cities, the steady deterioration in urban areas caused by neglect, and the rapid influx of industry to support the war effort, created an "urban crisis" far outstripping the single problem of the slums. The sad state of the nation's cities after the war created the background for the most significant housing legislation ever passed—the Housing Act of 1949. It was in this Act that Congress declared the goal of a "decent home and suitable living environment for every American family." Title I of the Act created the Urban Renewal Program —a recognition that entire areas of cities needed redevelopment, not just housing. Along with the creation of Urban Renewal went a new commitment to public housing. The Act authorized the construction of 810,000 new public housing units over the next six years— a goal not achieved until 1970.

This lack of follow-through on the lofty goal in the 1949 Act was caused by congressional penury and local prejudices, as well as the growing unpopularity of the public housing program. The Eisenhower Administration was cool to the concept of public housing. The Commissioner of the Public Housing Administration expressed his reservations openly. An Advisory Committee on Government Housing in 1953 laid stress on rehabilitation of existing homes: "We must restore to sound condition all dwellings worth saving." The Committee also authored the concept of the "Workable Program for Community Improvement," which made local codes and ordinances a prerequisite for federal assistance. Even if the stated goal of the Workable Program to have localities "help themselves" was authentic, the result was that most communities now had a legal reason for *not* participating in the public housing program.

Part of the cause of the congressional cut-backs in appropriations was that the public housing population was beginning to change—from what one writer labeled the "submerged middle class," mostly whites, to primarily black, fatherless families on public assistance. Thus, political support waned and was reflected in Congress.

The federal government, however, did focus its concern on the housing problems of the elderly. In 1956, Congress provided for the admission of single, elderly persons into public housing, gave extra subsidy funds to local authorities for the benefit of elderly tenants, and authorized higher construction costs for their specially designed houses.

This concern for the elderly carried over into the Housing Act of 1959, the next significant step in the legislative process. That Act established three new housing programs for the elderly, including the Section 202 program of direct loans at low interest to non-profit sponsors of housing for senior citizens.

The brief success with the "202" Program of below-market interest loans laid the groundwork for a new departure in 1961.

President John F. Kennedy stated in his Housing and Community Development Message on March 9, 1961:

> In 1949, Congress with great vision announced our national policy of "a decent home and a suitable living environment for every American family." We have progressed since that time; but, we must still redeem this pledge to the 14 million American families who currently live in substandard or deteriorating homes, and protect the other 19 million American families from the environment of blight and slums.

To "redeem this pledge," the Kennedy Administration pressed for enactment of the Housing Act of 1961. It contained the first truly innovative housing program for families since the U. S. Housing Act of 1937—the Section 221 (d) (3) FHA program for moderate income families. Because of the success with the Section 202 direct loan program for the *elderly*, which allowed nonprofit organizations to be sponsors, the Congress decided to let nonprofit and limited dividend sponsors receive below-market interest rate loans for projects designed for moderate income *families*.

The 221 (d) (3) program was significant because of its enlistment of private sponsors, and, also, its attempt to assist persons just above the income level eligible for public housing—those unable to qualify for public housing or able to buy or rent on the open market.

These new dimensions of federal housing policy laid the foundation for the next important legislative landmark—the Rent Supplement Program. President Lyndon B. Johnson, in his Message on the Cities in 1965, called the Rent Supplement Program "the most crucial instrument in our effort to improve the American city." Because of the positive experience with the 221 (d) (3) program, private sponsorship and management was encouraged in the provision of FHA-insured housing for low-income families, those within the public housing income levels. The family would pay 25 percent of its income for rent, and the federal government would pay the remainder required for the market rental. As the tenant's income rose, his rent would increase—he would not have to move out, as in public housing.

Despite these new "instruments" for providing housing forged in 1961 and 1965, production was not very high. Nearly 200,000 units have been built under each program. Four hundred thousand units since 1961 is not dramatic.

Partly because of this paltry record, together with the dismal production level of public housing, which was at about 35,000 units per year in the mid 1960's, leaders in the housing industry and those groups representing citizens in need of housing began to call for a much more substantial effort. Both the Kerner Commission on Civil Disorders and the Kaiser Committee on Urban Housing called for specific national goals and thought in terms of six million units needed by low and moderate income families.

Many important voices such as these converged in 1968, and influenced the passage of the most far-reaching housing act in our history—the Housing and Urban Development Act of 1968. President Johnson, in front of the HUD building in Washington, said expansively, "The Act can be the Magna Carta to liberate our Cities." This Act reaffirmed the 1949 Act's goal of a decent home and suitable living environment for every American family, and for the first time Congress stated a national goal of 26 million new housing units to be constructed in the next ten years.

Six million of these homes were to be built for the nation's ill-housed. But, could the existing programs do the job? Congress thought not, and created two new programs which were to become well known for their productivity, as well as for their controversy— the "236" program for rental housing and the "235" program for home-ownership. Both programs featured an interest subsidy concept which allowed the home buyer or renter to benefit from a monthly payment based on one percent interest on the mortgage. Eligible families were those earning one-third above the public housing income limits, that is $4000 to $8000.

The pressures on the federal budget caused by the Vietnam War necessitated a private source of the mortgages rather than government sources. Thus, the Federal National Mortgage Association was "privatized," and, 236 and 235 mortgages had to be made by private mortgage lenders. In addition, such groups as the Kaiser

Committee and Douglas Commission had released reports in 1968, calling for new emphasis on private sector involvement in housing.[1] For the first time in the history of housing legislation, the National Association of Home Builders and the National Association of Real Estate Boards joined in support of a housing bill for lower-income families.

These two programs accounted for the greatest acceleration of housing production for lower-income families in our history. From 1968 through 1972, 1,665,000 units of subsidized housing were produced—more than was produced in the thirty years after the U. S. Housing Act of 1937. In 1970 and 1971 combined, one out of every five new housing units produced was directly subsidized. This clearly contributed to the all-time housing production record of 2,581,000 units created in 1971. Production went even higher in 1972, as the federal assistance programs accounted for nearly one quarter of all starts. The housing industry was given a substantial boost, and millions of persons were living in decent homes they could afford.

Private investment in subsidized housing was greatly enhanced by the Tax Reform Act of 1969, which specifically exempted 236 and 221 (d) (3) housing from normal recapture penalties when rapid depreciation formulas were used by the owners on their federal income tax returns.

In addition to the incentives for private investment, these new subsidy programs were not put under local government control. Congress did not require a "workable program" as with public housing and 221 (d) (3). Nor did it require local government consent, as with the Rent Supplement program.

Most important, Congress appropriated the funds to implement what it had authorized, which was a radical departure from the past.

This production came to an abrupt halt on January 8, 1973, when the Nixon Administration imposed its moratorium on all housing subsidy programs.

HUD Secretary George Romney was drafted by Nixon to be the messenger of the demise of federally assisted housing programs. A few months later, the new Secretary, James Lynn, explained to a House Committee that "The reason that the suspension has been instituted is the mounting evidence that the present program structure we now have cannot yield effective results even with the most professional management."

The Nixon and Ford Administrations' view of housing policy

13

rests on the premise that past programs have failed. "The Federally subsidized housing approach has failed," President Nixon said on September 19, 1973.

Nixon further articulated the fundamental reason for the "failure."

> The main flaw . . . in the old approach is its underlying assumption that the basic problem of the poor is a lack of housing rather than a lack of income. Instead of treating the root cause of the problem—the inability to pay for housing—the Government has been attacking the symptom. We have been helping the builders directly and the poor only indirectly, rather than providing assistance directly to low-income families.

On the basis of this reasoning the Administration put forward a new approach—direct cash assistance.

> Under this approach, instead of providing a poor family with a place to live, the Federal Government would provide qualified recipients with an appropriate housing payment and would let them choose their own homes on the private market. The payment would be carefully scaled to make up the difference between what a family could afford on its own for housing and the cost of safe and sanitary housing in that geographic area. This plan would give the poor the freedom and responsibility to make their own choice about housing.

The President then concluded, ". . . of the policy alternatives available the most promising way to achieve decent housing for all of our families at an acceptable cost appears to be direct cash allowances."[2]

The Administration's housing allowance concept was framed to counter the alleged weaknesses of the federal subsidy programs. It is argued that the housing allowance system is *less expensive* and *more equitable*. That is, more persons will be assisted for less money. Also it is argued that freedom of housing choice will be enhanced, since recipients can live where they want to, not in specific housing sites tied to a subsidy program.

The Administration's strategy in implementing the new plan was very cautious. As outlined by the President in the September 19 Message, the first priority was to analyze the information gained from the experiment involving 18,000 families authorized in 1970 by Congress, and then to expand the experimental effort in 1974. A final decision as to the merits of the plan was to be made in late 1974 or early 1975. The next phase would be to try the new plan with the elderly poor. So, the plan would not be fully operative until 1976 or 1977. Insiders in Washington reported that the Office of Management and Budget was responsible for the extremely cautious approach.

Thus, as a result of the HUD study and the recommendations that were made to the President, HUD proposed a housing allowance program. They had Senator John Tower introduce it into the Senate in the fall of 1973. It would work like this—they would first experiment with helping elderly poor people, then expand it to poor people in general, and then if it worked, they would try to make it available to all the needy for housing. HUD officials thought that the Section 23 program, because it involved assistance payments to tenants in private dwellings, had a resemblance to housing allowances. Section 23 refers to an amendment to the public housing law made in 1965 which for the first time allowed the local housing authority to subsidize tenants living in *private* accommodations. As envisioned by its sponsor, Representative William Widnall, the program was to allow "scattered site" housing to be utilized so that subsidized families would not be concentrated in "projects" nor would neighbors near the scattered sites know about the subsidization by the local housing authority.

In practice, Section 23 did not work out like Widnall expected. HUD legal counselors were able to pressure local housing authorities to enter into "agreements to lease" private housing not yet constructed. When the housing was in fact constructed, then the lease would take effect. With the "agreement to lease" in hand, the private developer could get financing for the construction of the housing.

HUD's legal counselors were not trying to subvert the law; rather, they were creatively making it work, for it soon became evident that landlords were not coming forth with "scattered sites" to lease to local authorities. Most public housing level families are large, needing three or four bedrooms. They are usually black. Few landlords cater to either. Thus, it became necessary to find a way to get *new* housing via the Section 23 mechanism, and the HUD lawyers did it by the "agreement to lease" instrument.

But in his September 19 Message President Nixon pictured the Section 23 program as Representative Widnall had intended it to function. The President said he was satisfied that the Section 23 program has the characteristics the Administration looked for in a housing program, namely: it makes maximum use of existing housing, the government does not determine where projects are to be located, it involves a transfer payment rather than helping de-

15

velopers and builders and it is less costly. Therefore, the Administration put its stamp of approval on the Section 23 program.

Academically, the subject of housing allowance is not very important because it was not passed and it is not likely to be passed in the foreseeable future. Still the shuffles, arguments, and rhetorical flourishes by HUD had an impact because they were used by HUD officials to justify Section 23. As a consequence, HUD had a position from which to compromise its rigid idea of the housing allowance, which was not likely to get anywhere in Congress. HUD officials had a position from which they could say they would allow leased housing to be *the* housing program. On the other hand, it allowed Senators and House Members to say publicly, well at least we got some production out of the Administration. It was a point at which they could all agree that here was a program which might be acceptable. It was the substance of the compromise which allowed the Housing and Community Development Act of 1974 to be passed.

The Administration has since shunted aside the housing allowance program. Politically speaking, there was something disingenuous about the proposal made by HUD because it was so tentative and experimental and involved a very small amount of money. It made one think that HUD really did not want to spend anything on housing since it would be experimenting in 1974 and 1975, and 1976 would be an election year; in 1977 someone else would be in the White House, so it really did not matter. It looked like public relations flim flam. From his public statements it was clear Lynn did not want any housing—including Section 23 leasing. The government ought not to be involved in housing, he thought. He believed in the filter-down system as the way to provide housing for the lower-income families.

What HUD wanted was the Community Development program and if it could get Community Development passed by giving Congress leased housing, then that was an acceptable bone to throw.

Let us back up a moment and look at the Senate and House bills which were proposed in 1974, along with HUD's "Better Communities Act" and the Housing Allowance proposal.

On March 11, 1974, the Senate, on a 76-11 vote, passed the Housing and Community Development Act of 1974.

As far as housing is concerned, the bill called for a continuation of 235 and 236 under new Sections 402 and 502, with several reforms:

- Subsidy funds would be reserved for communities to meet the housing objectives contained in the applications approved under the new Community Development program, or would be made available for developers only for use on sites which generally conform to housing plans of units of general local governments.

- Prototype mortgage ceilings would be established to insure a more equitable distribution of subsidy funds to high cost areas.
- Eligibility for assistance would be limited in general to families with incomes less than 90 percent of median to insure more coverage for lower income families.
- Mandatory counseling would be required for Section 402 families and discretionary counseling for Section 502 families to reduce defaults.
- Rehabilitation would be encouraged by setting aside 20 percent of Section 502 funds for this purpose.
- Consumer protection would be increased by a warranty requirement and by provision for reimbursement for defective workmanship.
- Economic integration would be encouraged by requiring that 20 percent of rental units in each project be provided additional assistance payments on behalf of low-income families and that each project has a reasonable range of family income.
- Special consideration for the elderly would be attained by requiring that from 15 percent of contract for rental assistance payments be set aside for housing projects for the elderly.
- Improved management would be fostered by authorizing the Secretary to provide through contracts or otherwise for monitoring and supervising of privately sponsored projects.
- Additional subsidies would be authorized under Section 502 to meet bona fide rising operating costs. Rents would be at least 25 percent of net income, and no rent would be less than the cost of utilities.

The bill also strongly supported the Public Housing leasing program along traditional lines.

Section 802 of the Senate Bill gave authority to HUD to expand the experimental Housing Allowance Program, and asked for a report eight months after enactment.

So, it is obvious that the Senate differed deeply from the Administration's policy on housing. The Senate wanted to improve the 236 and 235 programs as well as the Public Housing leasing program. The Administration did not want any semblance of 236 and 235. It wanted housing allowances, and only on an experimental basis. It also wanted a revised Section 23 program that looks as much like a housing allowance program as possible, for example, private

17

management and 20 percent or less units occupied by those on assistance.

The Administration, however, did want Community Development—the special revenue sharing program which consolidated Model Cities, Urban Renewal, Rehabilitation Loans and Grants, Concentrated Code Enforcement, Water and Sewer Grants, Neighborhood Facilities Construction, and Public Facilities Loans. The issue was: the Administration wanted Community Development and experimental housing allowances; the Senate wanted Community Development *and* subsidized housing, and it wanted them connected. The Senate Report states that:

> All localities requesting Federal funds for significant local development *should be required* to fulfill certain minimum standards relative to providing decent housing and eliminating slums and blight.

The Senate bill reflected the view expressed by Senator Adlai Stevenson to Secretary Lynn:

> I think the main point, Mr. Secretary, is that it is very difficult for us to consider housing and community development as if each were separate from the other. They simply are not. Housing is part of community development.

Support for the housing bill passed by the Senate was expressed by most housing groups, including the National Housing Conference, the National Association of Home Builders, and the National Association of Housing and Redevelopment Officials.

HUD, however, released a statement saying that although the bill contained many "improvements" it also "contains a disjointed, overlapping potpourri of subsidized housing and community development features." Secretary Lynn threatened to recommend a veto, if a bill "substantially like" the Senate bill reached the White House.

HUD was counting on getting a more compatible bill from the House, where a housing and community development bill passed on June 20, 1974.

The House of Representatives

In 1973 and early 1974, HUD spokesmen were adamant in their opposition to anything but their own Community Development Bill and the housing allowance experiment. Likewise, Congressional spokesmen were strong in their support of their own measure. Efforts to pass housing legislation began with the omnibus

House Bill (H.R. 10036), sponsored by Representatives Barrett and Ashley. The bill proposed, like the Senate's, "to bolster the undertaking of housing and community development activities in a coordinated and mutually supportive manner" (Section 101 (4)). But the key characteristic of the House Bill was that housing funds would go directly to *units of local government* for distribution to housing developers, owners, and renters.

The House Bill was bold in its approach to both Community Development and Housing and clear in its attempt to combine the two.

However, the threat of impeachment proceedings in Congress and the memory of 1972, when an omnibus housing bill faltered because of its complexity, caused the Subcommittee on Housing, led by Barrett and Ashley, to reduce the housing legislation to a "bobtail" bill.

The "bobtail" bill, worked out with HUD officials, abandoned all subsidized housing except Section 23 leasing. The bill would allow HUD to allocate funds directly to local governments, which would then select the developers. The Section 235 and 236 programs would be continued only in order to meet bona fide commitments established by HUD at the time of the suspension. The bill passed the House by a 351 to 25 vote.

The Senators on the Conference Committee fought hard to keep the 235 and 236 programs alive, but the resistance from HUD and the House Members was formidable. In return for the "bone" of the new leasing program (now labeled "Section 8"), the Senators went along with the "bobtail" bill—which ultimately became the Housing and Community Development Act of 1974.

A Defense Against the Attack on Subsidized Housing Programs: Burke teaches Nixon

With the history of housing legislation now outlined, it is possible to put the Nixon Administration's attack on the subsidized housing programs in some perspective—a very critical one as far as I am concerned.

Although Secretary Romney played "Samson" on January 8, 1973 by pulling down the whole edifice of subsidized housing, he was really the dispensable soldier in an all-out war on housing.

The President and Secretary Lynn continued the war by a steady barrage of condemnatory speeches in early 1973.

The housing subsidy programs are too *costly* was the refrain. President Nixon said in his State of the Union Message on Community Development on March 8, 1973, that "the old and wasteful programs, programs which have already obligated the taxpayers to payments of *between $63 and $95 billion* during the next forty years, are not the answer."

Secretary Lynn added his voice to this budgetary argument on March 15, 1973, when he said, "The real issue is fiscal responsibility versus either more inflation or more taxes. . . . Too many of the programs that were begun in the name of compassion have failed. It is far more compassionate to hold the line against inflation."

The "excessive cost" attack on subsidized housing programs can be defended against on several counts.

First, the total cost of the subsidy programs is wildly exaggerated by means of a simple multiplication sleight of hand. Mr. Nixon's speech writers multiplied the current *annual* subsidy amounts forty times the term of the mortgages, to come up with the $95 billion in the State of the Union Message. A key characteristic of the FHA subsidy programs, however, is that as incomes rise so do rents paid by tenants. As the tenants pay more, the government pays less. Simply allowing for the inflation factor, income of subsidized tenants should rise to a nonsubsidized level in ten to twelve years. Therefore, the figures of Mr. Nixon are *four* times the actual fact!

Second, the "excessive cost" argument usually leaves out the economic *benefits* created by the expenditures. New housing projects generate jobs, services, revenue of property taxes by local and state governments, and a general stimulus to the economy—a stimulus which results in an increased collection of federal taxes.

Third, cutting back on housing subsidies as a measure against inflation is contradictory and in itself *inflationary*. Since the fundamental fact about housing in America is that there is not enough of it, the demand is greater then the supply. To stop increasing the supply, while the growth of population increases the demand, is to create still greater inflationary pressures on the housing market. Inevitably, a slowdown in housing production helps to raise the price of housing and penalize the housing consumer.

For instance, while the housing moratorium has been in effect, the average price of a new home in our country as risen from $30,500 to $37.600. So, while the Administration fought inflation by stopping housing, the cost of a house went up over 23 percent!

Fourth, the "excessive cost" argument is an unfair attack on the lower-income beneficiaries of housing assistance, because each year the federal government provides indirect housing subsidies to middle and upper income homeowners by means of the deduction of mortgage interest payments which total more than the direct subsidies to the poor—about $6.8 billion versus $2.1 billion, as of 1973.

It is not difficult to predict the reaction to a "moratorium" by the IRS on all deductions from income of interest payments. Many families would not be able to afford a home, just as millions of lower-income families cannot now buy or rent a decent home.

Fifth, the proponents of the "excessive cost" argument usually have another "less expensive" way of providing housing in mind, for instance, a cash housing allowance system. We have already argued that the costs of the current subsidy programs are exaggerated, and when the true costs are compared to the figures put forward as the costs of a housing allowance system, the differences are not significant. As Anthony Downs says:

> There is no way to fully meet either the Nation's physical or financial housing needs without spending about this amount (five to seven billion dollars) annually for direct housing subsidies. This would be true even if the form of subsidy were shifted entirely to a housing allowance.[3]

To the economic justification for the freeze, the Administration has added that the housing programs are bad from a *policy* point of view. Lynn somewhat backtracked on his budgetary argument to emphasize his view of the housing programs' failure, when he appeared before a Senate committee in July 1973.

SENATOR TAFT: Mr. Secretary, do you feel that there is basis for the claim that housing, in effect, is being held hostage to inflation?

MR. LYNN: I think the principal reason for the suspension of the housing subsidized programs is our assessment of the inequities and the waste of those programs.

It was of these policy objections that the Secretary promised to speak, when he said HUD would evaluate the programs during the moratorium. On September 19, 1973, President Nixon said, "Six months ago, in my State of the Union Message on Community Development, I announced a sweeping study of Federal housing policy. . . . That study has been completed—and my recommendations are ready."

The "sweeping study" mentioned by the President was published on October 6, 1973, and was entitled, *Housing in the Seventies*. As was expected, it focused on the "inequities" and "waste" of the Federal housing subsidy programs.

The theme of the Report is that federal housing laws are "replete with inconsistencies, conflicts, and obsolete provisions and are without overall design or coordinated structure." Such laws were enacted, the Report says, without "study or revaluation of the relevant policies and legislative authorities." The laws reflected Congress' "own interests and notions as well as the pleadings of special interest groups." Furthermore, Congress enacted the laws with "little consideration of the economic and social costs and benefits, the equity aspects and the overall impact on local housing markets of subsidizing large numbers of newly built units for lower income families."

The negative results of such laws are insurmountable, the writers conclude.

> Government subsidized housing programs contain structural problems that result in considerable program inequities and inefficiencies. Certain problems could be remedied through legislative changes. However, legislative correction of one problem would often tend to aggravate or create others. More importantly, while administrative changes would marginally improve the efficiency and equity of production programs, serious problems of inefficiency and inequity in using production as the basic approach would remain. (P. 4-22)

What are these inequities and inefficiences which render production subsidies hopeless of improvement?

The recurrent appeal to "inequity" is based on the number of persons served by the subsidy programs.

> The Section 235 homeownership program has not made significant progress toward achieving equity. Only 12.6 percent of the families served have incomes of less than $5,000 annually. . . . In the income class with greatest participation ($6,000 to $6,999) only 2.7 percent of eligible families are served. . . . The Section 236 program serves less than one percent of all households earning less than $8000 per year. (P. 4-23)

Here, we have two programs enacted in 1968, getting really under way in 1969-72, producing more housing than all other programs combined in our nation's history, abruptly terminated by HUD, and, then, accused by HUD writers of not serving enough of the persons intended to be served by the programs! Is it really logical to say, since we are not helping *all*, let's help *none*?

Unfortunately, this seems to be a case of follow the leader. Secretary Lynn often decried the "widespread inequity" of the housing subsidy program. To a meeting in Boston he said,

> The total number of people actually assisted—either in public housing or in other federally subsidized houses or apartments —was little over six million. This is less than a quarter of the 24½ million Americans living on incomes below (the) official low-income line.

In addition to the illogic of such arguments—to stop the housing programs because they have not served everyone—Lynn's statement is subject to correction on its merits. The Senior Specialist in Housing at the Library of Congress, Henry S. Schechter (now housing advisor at the AFL/CIO), has provided such a correction:

> Among the 24½ million persons below the low-income line there are some 2.6 million unrelated individuals (i.e., outside of families) who are under 65 years of age. Non-elderly persons under 62 are not eligible for subsidized housing. This would reduce to about 22 million the number of low-income persons for whom housing assistance might be intended. At the same time . . . the HUD study states: "Almost 2.8 million dwelling units have been provided since 1937 through Government subsidized programs for low and moderate income families." At a conservatively estimated three person household size, a total of 8.4 million people would be served.[4]

Schechter adds to this correction of Lynn's figures the further point that many of these low-income families do not *need* new housing.

> In 1970, for example, there were 5,292,000 *households* in owner-occupied homes who had incomes of less than $4,000. Many of these homes were, no doubt, substandard, but many of them were not substandard. . . . It does not follow that they were being inequitably treated if they did not receive a subsidy for housing.[5]

And, Schechter concludes, Lynn's figures do not take into account that the federal government also made $2.6 billion in welfare payments to state and local governments, which was used by welfare recipients for housing.

So, again, we find figures are fudged and logic is abandoned in the attack on housing subsidies.

Program Viability

Finally, the writers of *Housing in the Seventies* apply the standard of "program viability" to the subsidized housing programs.

Again, the "facts" conform to previous remarks by Secretary Lynn. In September of 1973, he said,

> Our projections indicate that some nineteen percent of the Section 235 subsidized houses and twenty percent of the Section 236 subsidized apartments will be foreclosed upon default within the next decade.

The writers of the report accurately tracked the Secretary:

> Approximately thirty percent of all . . . Rent Supplement projects and twenty percent of all Section 236 projects are projected to fail during their first ten years. . . . About sixteen percent of all Section 235 homes will fail during their first ten years.[6]

The basis for these projections is the experience of FHA's unsubsidized programs and of the Section 221 (d) (3) below market interest rate program.

Schechter provides some interesting insight in response to the charges that the programs are not viable from an economic perspective. Much to HUD's chagrin, Schechter points out that criminal activities on the part of FHA officials "were a major factor in high Section 235 foreclosure rates. The HUD study and Secretary Lynn ignore this factor in assessing program viability." He goes on to say, "As a result of 'cleaning up' and tightened surveillance by HUD, the program failure rate should be much lower."[7]

It is sobering to consider that a year-long study of federal housing subsidy programs would overlook the most publicized aspect of them—poor administration by HUD. In 1974, the newspapers carried reports of investigations of FHA offices in twenty major cities. The Joint Economic Committee of Congress found poor administration to be the major cause of high default in the subsidy programs.[8]

Suspicion of avoiding the real issue is naturally aroused when the arguments propounded are so thin—as almost every analyst agrees in the case of the freeze on housing.

A good summary of these analyses is contained in a report, *Federal Housing Subsidies: Their Nature and Effectiveness and What We Should Do About Them*, by Anthony Downs, an eminent real estate researcher. His report concludes:

> On balance, we believe that both the Section 235 and Section 236 programs are effective instruments for meeting the key objectives of housing subsidies. The major inadequacies so far encountered in execution of these programs have stemmed

24

mainly from either poor administration by HUD or the inherently higher risks of investing capital in housing for relatively low-income households in relatively deteriorated areas.

A preponderant majority of the more than one-half million housing units made available under these programs have been well received by both their occupants and the surrounding communities.

. . . Initial experience indicates that a significant percentage of households who start receiving those subsidies earn their way out of them through higher income.

The fact that these programs provide profitable incentives for builders and investors to undertake them is an advantage, not a disadvantage. It stimulates participation of private capital, and has helped generate vastly greater production of subsidized units than ever before.[9]

The real worth of federally subsidized housing can be tested only be observing the tangible improvement in people's living conditions. Although there have been some housing complexes poorly located, or badly managed, or improperly constructed, the multitude of successes illustrates that nothing inherently causes them to fail. For instance, in Dallas, Texas, a 280-unit Rent Supplement community called Colonia Tepeyac is a model of cleanliness and beautiful design. Five years after its completion it looks sparkling and the residents are proud of their home. They would laugh at the words of the HUD writers that they have a 30 percent chance to fail!

Since the leaders of HUD and the writers of the Policy Review omitted the most obvious criticism of the subsidy program—poor administration—and offered up arguments against the programs which, as Downs says, "have proven to be either false or capable of being responded to effectively without fundamental changes in program design," then it appears that other reasons lay behind their attack on housing.

President Nixon himself gave a hint of the reason in his September 19 message, when, in supporting a housing allowance system, he said, "It would eventually get the Federal Government out of the housing business."

Is this, after all, the meaning of the war on housing—to get the federal government out of the housing field? Is this not what lies behind the cavalier treatment in the HUD report of the legislation which was thirty years in developing?

25

To the Samsons of the Nixon Administration, we need to bring the prudent words of Edmund Burke, who advised, "*It is with infinite caution that any man ought to venture upon pulling down an edifice, which has answered in any tolerable degree . . . the common purposes of society.*"[10] Burke was, of course, referring to the "edifice" of the State, but still his words can make us sensitive to the danger of radical action, with respect to any part of our national patrimony.

Perhaps the critics of the Congress with its "inconsistencies," its listening to "special pleadings," could be gently taught by Burke's caution:

> We are but too apt to consider things in the state which we find them, without sufficiently adverting to the causes by which they have been produced, and possibly may be upheld. . . . No man should approach to look into (the state's) defects or corruptions but with due caution, . . . he should never dream of beginning its reformation by its subversion; . . . he should approach to the faults of the state as to the wounds of a father with pious awe and trembling solicitude. By this wise prejudice we are taught to look with horror on those children of this country, who are prompt rashly to hack that aged parent in pieces, and put him into the kettle of magicians, in hopes that their poisonous weeds, and wild incantations, they may regenerate the paternal constitution, and rennovate their father's life.[11]

I myself admit to some "prejudice"—I hope in the Burkean sense—about our legislative heritage. For two years, I worked each day as a small part of that large whole which makes up our national legislature. No one will deny that bad laws are sometimes passed, but neither will any one with acquaintance deny the arduous path of a legislative measure, nor fail to be impressed with the actuality of enactment. So to contemplate the demise of a program which surely contains substantial benefits to the citizenry conjures a dreadful vision. As Burke said, "Time is required to produce that union of minds which alone can produce all the good we aim at."[12] Or, as he poetically described it:

> By a slow but well sustained progress, the effect of each step is watched; the good or ill success of the first give light to us in the second; and so, from light to light, we are conducted with safety through the whole series. We see that the parts of the system do not clash. The evils latent in the most promising contrivances are provided for as they rise. One advantage is as little as possible sacrificed to another. We compensate, we rec-

oncile, we balance. We are enabled to unite into a consistent whole the various anomalies and contending principles that are found in the minds and affairs of men. From hence arises, not an excellence in simplicity, but one far superior, an excellence in composition.[13]

It is not a pleasant discovery, if correct, that those in a position to lead the Department of Housing and Urban Development do not cherish what their predecessors labored to build. A long host of compassionate persons fought many battles to build the edifice of housing programs—Robert Wagner, Leon Keyserling, Franklin Roosevelt, Robert Taft, Albert Rains, Charles Abrams, Robert Weaver, John Sparkman, and Lyndon Johnson. We depend on the people who are given the burden of power to respond to the needs of their fellow citizens, and to preserve and protect their tenuous legacies of justice. It remains true, as Burke said two centuries ago,

> though it may seem paradoxical; but in general, those who are habitually employed in finding and displaying faults, are unqualified for the work of reformation: because their minds are not only unfurnished with patterns of the fair and good, but by habit they come to take no delight in the contemplation of those things.[14]

II. HOUSING THE ILL-HOUSED:
PUBLIC HOUSING IN AMERICA

Although most Americans tend to lump all government-assisted housing under the name "public housing" there is a specific "public housing" program, as distinguished from the FHA-subsidized programs and the Section 8 leasing program enacted in 1974.

"Public Housing" is, strictly speaking, the shelter provided for poor families by local housing authorities. These local bodies, usually run by a Board of Commissioners, own and operate housing which is financed by bonds on which the U.S. Government guarantees the debt service. The rents are set at very low rates because the federal government also delivers an annual subsidy to the housing authority to pay off the bonds.

The public housing program was established in 1937 by the U.S. Housing Act.

Public Housing

The major theme of Public Housing was economic—an attempt to get the nation back on its feet and out of the Depression. The program was therefore an economic one, and not a housing program as such. No thought was given to its permanency until the constituency of Public Housing became permanent rather than temporary. Then all kinds of ramifications developed, involving racial change and transient tenants.

Public Housing has the image of being occupied almost totally by minorities. When it first started it was almost 100 percent white. I met one of the fathers of the City of Corpus Christi who had engineered getting Public Housing for Corpus Christi in the days of Roosevelt. He thought he was the first one in the country able to get housing for minorities as well as for the whites. He was able to do it by building three projects: one for whites, one for blacks, and one for Mexican Americans! In that time and in that context, it was a forward move. Namely, they built some housing for people other then the submerged middle class white family.

Public housing is a federally funded but locally operated program. The federal law requires States to pass enabling legislation granting powers to local governments to establish the program. All fifty states have such legislation. There are more than 3000 local housing authorities, operating over a million units—from the rural town with one small project to the New York City Housing Authority with 170,000 units.

The U. S. Housing Act requires that a local housing authority enter into a cooperation agreement with the city. The agreement states that property of the LHA shall be exempt from *ad valorem* taxes and that the city will provide the usual municipal services. Most agreements also call for a payment in lieu of taxes to the city, usually equal to 10 percent of the tenants' rents.

Until the 1960's, public housing was the only program to help alleviate the problems of the ill-housed in America. Throughout its history it has been pummeled by criticism from real estate interests who saw it as a competitive threat and by spokesmen for the poor who resented the regimentation and drabness of the projects.

Lawrence Friedman, in *Government and Housing*, does the best job of describing the conflicts and difficulties in public housing. He coined the phrase "submerged middle class." This emphasized who the first occupants of public housing were, and who are no longer the main occupants. Today the main occupants of public housing are the poor, black, predominantly fatherless families. That is the case because there is a large amount of public housing in the big cities.

A significant number of the public housing projects are still located in the small towns in America, with basically a white and elderly complexion.

The changes in public housing were the result of the transformation of the constituency. All of a sudden, the public housing projects which were built in the 30's and 40's for fairly well-behaved, submerged middle class families were emptied out and filled up with a mostly black, fatherless, misbehaving constituency, with attendant social maladjustments, which led to crimes and vandalism, and social disorder in every large city in the country. Nonwhite occupancy in public housing increased from 43 percent in 1954 to 53 percent in 1964.

It is difficult to think of a city which has not had some severe difficulties in public housing. Every ardent opponent to public housing always introduces Pruitt-Igoe in St. Louis as the transparent symbol of all the public housing ever built in the country. That project is instructive for us. The architects who designed Pruitt-Igoe designed for the submerged middle class as its occupants. They got caught in the squeeze; a different type of person and family there than they had expected, so the place did not work.

As a positive result of facing the failures like Pruitt-Igoe, significant changes were begun in the 1960's in the whole public housing enterprise. HUD began to require that, if at all financially feasible, high rise buildings were not to be constructed. This did not apply to elderly projects, which are still allowed, because the social disorder is not present. Elderly people should be near community facilities within the city which are not available near lower-priced land.

The major horror stories came out of situations where the housing was built in the 40's and 50's and then the population changed. A truer picture of public housing would show that very few high rise structures have been built in the inner city in the 60's and 70's except for the elderly.

With the Act of 1956, the first glimmerings of change in attitude toward design of public housing could be seen. In 1937, while constructing a program for people who would be temporary residents, the amenities were not stressed as much as sturdiness. It is appalling to realize that some of the projects built in the late 30's and 40's did not have walls for the bathrooms or closets, only rods for curtains. Of course, they are not air conditioned, and have no trim to speak of, but were just concrete block construction.

In the 50's, when the problems of the elderly became important and more building for the elderly was initiated, more money was alloted on each unit. Congressmen themselves started calling for improvements in the design of public housing. This did not really catch on until about 1961 when Marie McGuire became the head of public housing. She had been the head of the San Antonio Housing Authority, and was quite concerned about the design of Public Housing. She instituted a program of design awards and fought for special amenities such as balconies, ramps, dining rooms, and social services. A Congressman from New York, James Scheuer, who had been involved in the Urban Renewal program in Southwest Washington, also began to champion the cause of better design against continuous opposition. Some people continued to believe that public housing should have only the barest necessities, and agreed with a General Accounting Office report in 1962 which argued that money spent for balconies was profligate. Once consciousness came that public housing was not temporary, however, changes began to be made.

It was insufficient merely to put a person in a new and clean house or apartment. A home should also have some beauty. This idea was slow in catching on and has not peaked yet, but there has been improvement because of the change in constituency and the efforts of persons such as Marie McGuire and James Scheuer to make public housing more attractive.

In contrast to the Pruitt-Igoes of public housing, there are many truly successful ventures where residents enjoy their home. Wise House, a twenty-story complex on the West Side of Manhattan, where families of varied income levels, different ages, and several racial and ethnic backgrounds live together, is one example. Another is Ping Yuan, a medium rise apartment house in San Francisco's Chinatown. It is strikingly attractive architectually, and the lively morale of residents is evident.

A student of mine, Keimi Harada, listed these points for success in public housing:

1. Physical	Good Site Selection
	Attractive Architecture
	High Quality Construction
2. Social Aspect	Racial Integration
	Mixture of Family-Income Types
3. Institutional Aspect	Local Government Initiative

Turnkey

The movement to get the public officials out of the business of supervising and building public housing came in 1966. A building plan designed by a committee is like the committe that started out to build a horse and came up with a camel. It is unfortunately true that public architecture is of lesser quality than private.

Ada Louise Huxtable,[1] America's leading architectural critic, believes the Boston City Hall is an excellently designed public building. She thinks that one of the reasons for such a masterpiece is that the city had a competition. They advertised all over the world, and some very young unknown architects won the competition and designed the City Hall. This is a process opposite to the normal way of building city halls or housing projects in this country.

It seemed to have a beneficial effect on the design and construction of public housing when, in 1966, the Turnkey program was instituted by HUD. The design and construction of public housing by and large was put into the private sector. Public housing authorities still had their review and comment process, but the burden was on the private architect and developer to design and build the housing, a change which has been extremely beneficial.

The motivation for Turnkey and Leasing, however, was not design. It was to find a way to pare the cost, the time, and the

31

government red tape. The move to privatize the design and construction of public housing began in 1965 with the passage of the leasing section of the housing act, Section 23. The regulations put out in 1966 allowed leased housing to be newly constructed and a turnkey method was conceived by Joseph Burstein, a HUD lawyer.

Eventually Turnkey became the major method of constructing public housing. The fact that there was very little debate in Congress about the wisdom of Turnkey is testimony to its effectiveness. This changeover has cut in half the time it takes to build a public housing project.

In speaking of the various methods of financing, such as conventional, FHA financing, bond financing, as ways to build for Turnkey or leased housing, one should not overlook the very significant role of the states in the financing of public housing in the future. One of the most significant parts of the 1974 Act was a provision for the federal government to subsidize the interest on bonds sold by state housing authorities for the construction of housing projects. The point is that there is a fourth mechanism to finance public housing.

The homebuilders and apartment builders of the states are not doing well because the other mechanisms of financing are not available. In addition, the Housing and Community Development Act of 1974 subsidizes the enterprise of the State housing authority. That will be a strong incentive for every state to set up such an authority to finance housing under the only program available, Section 8 leasing.

Another important legislative impact on public housing has to do with the financing of the operation, not the financing of the development. When the U. S. Housing Act of 1937 was drafted, it embodied a very simple concept. The local housing authority would receive a subsidy, called an annual contribution, with which it would pay off its bonds. In other words, there would be no capital cost to the local authority. It was assumed, therefore, that the rents collected would pay for all the operations, administration, maintenance, and utilities. There were no propery taxes.

The rent formula was set up to defray normal operations of the projects, which was simple, but it had inherent difficulties. The public housing program required that income limits be placed on tenants. The Act stated that the rents charged at their maximum should be 20 percent less than the lowest charged in the community, the famous "20 percent gap." Those are fairly stern limitations.

The first housing authorities that were created in the 30's and 40's had an alternative of creating a flat rent. For example, a one

32

bedroom would rent for $20, a two bedroom for $30, three for $40, and so on, for anybody who lived there. To get in, a person had to meet the income requirements. On the other hand, the LHA had the alternative of charging strictly according to income. Thus, in a one bedroom there might be a young couple paying $30 or an old couple living on old age assistance paying only $10.

The flat rate system was used by many authorities but was largely abandoned because it seemed unfair. It seemed wrong for very poor people to pay the same rent as people not as poor. In reality they were all poor. Therefore, nearly all housing authorities adopted the system of charging rent according to income.

Beginning in the 50's and more so in the 60's, this whole process came head on into a formidable obstacle. Operational costs began outstripping the ability to collect the rents. Public housing authorities had to operate in the black, so they started taking in people who could pay more money, those at the top of the income limits. Thus, if rents were according to income, more money was collected. This had an adverse effect on many persons, especially the elderly. Even though the elderly person might earn $100 a month, the minimum rent might be $30, or 30 percent of their income. There were cases back in 1967 and 1968 where people were paying 60 and 70 percent of their income for rent. Housing authorities were in trouble because tenants were paying too high a percentage of their income in rent.

The agitation about this culminated in 1969, and finally in the Act of 1969, Senator Brooke took the lead, and sponsored what is now called the Brooke Amendment. This states that without exception, no family in public housing shall pay more than 25 percent of its income for rent. Obviously, that would bankrupt most of the housing authorities in this country, many of which were already in the red. Brooke said, in order to minimize the impact on the housing authorities, operating costs would be subsidized. For the first time it was recognized that the housing authorities' *operations*, as well as capital costs, needed to be subsidized.

The theory was good, and it passed in Congress, and money was authorized, but that is less than half of the job. Most of the job is getting the money appropriated. In this case, the Senators and Congressmen on the Appropriations Committee were faced with a request for approximately $100 million in the first year, and now close to $500 million, for operating subsidies. At first virtually nothing was appropriated. In 1972 they finally appropriated some money, but it was inadequate; likewise in 1973. Those housing

33

authorities which were already suffering because of the high cost of operation were literally going into bankruptcy. St. Louis even gave their projects back to the federal government, which would not accept them! They did finally reach a compromise where St. Louis would keep them, but HUD would provide extra money.

It can be said to the credit of the HUD officials that they admitted the concept of the operating subsidy and fought for a great increase in the 1974 Act. In the meantime, housing authorities had had to go into their replacement reserves, so now almost every housing authority in the United States is out of money in its replacement reserve. In five or six years or sooner, when refrigerators, fans, etc. have to be replaced, there will be no money to replace them.

The housing authorities had to find a way around the problem caused by the Brooke Amendment. So, they established what are called "bracket rents." They would take a project with 100 units: Assuming for simplicity that they all have two bedrooms, they would say that of these 100 units, 20 percent of the people will pay the maximum rent, for example $50, 30 percent pay $40, 30 percent pay $30, and 20 percent pay $10. They have thus guaranteed that they will not fill up the project with the lowest income people. They have also guaranteed that no one would pay more than 25 percent of his income. Under the Brooke Amendment, fantastic as it sounds, it is possible for the housing authority to pay somebody to live in one of its apartments. The reason for this is that with a certain income, a deduction of $300 is allowed for each child, and a blanket deduction for incidentals of 5 percent is also allowed. With the deductions, a person might have the effective income of zero, and would pay zero rent. In older projects, where the tenants pay the utilities, the housing authority would pay the utilities. It is possible, then, for a family to pay no rent and for the authority to pay the utilities. That is the kind of thing that would totally ruin a housing authority if it happened too often.

For survival, the housing authorities instituted the bracket rent concept, to avoid filling the project with the very poor people. There are some pitfalls which cannot be avoided. For example, a person previously paying $40 who become sick or disabled and cannot pay cannot be evicted, so his rent is lowered to zero. Also, a U. S. District Court in Pennsylvania ruled that the bracket rent system is unconstitutional. HUD has challenged this ruling and it is on appeal, though it has not yet gone to the appeals court. It is unconstitutional according to the argument that there is equal protection under the Constitution, that there cannot be discrimination according to income, and people have the right to equal benefit of public housing.

It is inevitable that the financial strains on public housing are causing the authorities to try to solve their problems by not helping the poorest people. Looked at from a legalistic point of view, that is wrong, but the authorities cannot be blamed for trying to stay financially solvent. 2005869

Landlord/tenant law has been affected by the public housing enterprise. In usual landlord/tenant relations, stated bluntly in common law terms, the tenant has no rights. The landlord may demand possession at any time without cause, even if the rent was paid ahead of time. Any justice of peace or any court in the United States will by and large grant the landlord that decision; that is a system that has held for centuries. Public housing for the first time gave the courts another perspective on the landlord/tenant relationship.

Congress has said that every family shall have a decent home and suitable living environment, and all persons in a certain income class were qualified and eligible for the benefits of this program. Then the Constitutional question comes in of how the benefits of the government can be denied to an individual. The insertion of that factor in the legal system has resulted in a whole series of cases which have established these principles: 1) No person in public housing can be evicted without due process. 2) No person in public housing can be evicted without cause. 3) No person can be evicted from public housing without some system of grievance set up by the local housing authority.

These are potent principles for a public housing authority to have to deal with, in contrast to the normal case, where the landlord simply demands possession. The Housing Authority has to be sure that it follows the procedure set up by the law. It must inform the person of the reason for eviction and give ten days notice to vacate the apartment. In those ten days, the tenant has the right of appeal, which can be set up in many ways. In most public housing projects there are grievance panels represented by tenants, management, and outsiders.

It appears that the Housing and Community Development Act of 1974 has rung down the curtain on the expansion of the public housing in America. HUD has effectively put forward the Section 8 leasing program as the only housing assistance program. Therefore, the challenge ahead for local housing authorities is to find ways to conserve their housing stock and to come up with new and effective ways to involve tenants in cooperating to make the housing a decent place to live.

Perhaps some local housing authorities will also find ways to use their inherent powers creatively. Many legal experts believe that under existing statutes the public housing authority could use its tax-exempt bonding power to back privately financed moderate income housing, so long as the land and improvements revert to the Public Housing Authority at the end of the mortgage term. If property tax exemptions were also granted by the city, then even lower-income families could be served. So a housing authority does not have to lie down and die even if it is abandoned by the federal government.

III. RENEWING THE CITIES:
URBAN RENEWAL

The Urban Renewal program was established by Section I of the Housing Act of 1949. The primary focus was on slum clearance, reminiscent of the U. S. Housing Act of 1937, which focused on housing programs, but also emphasized slum clearance in that each new unit of public housing had to replace a demolished slum house. That was completely impractical, and did not remain in the law very long. Slum clearance could not be achieved just by the housing program, but conceptually its achievement could be expected via a total redevelopment and slum clearance effort.

The idea prevailed that housing was not enough; that cities themselves were in a deplorable state after years of neglect and the War. The law provided assistance to localities to redevelop entire areas of cities.

Title I allowed the areas to be chosen by the cities. It allowed a similar legal operation that had been chosen for public housing. The city was permitted to establish a local renewal authority, or a local public authority, which would have the power of eminent domain. It would be eligible, if enabled by state legislation, to borrow money and to receive grants from the federal government and to engage in acquisition and disposition of land on behalf of redevelopment activities.

In a typical situation, five commissioners appointed by the mayor and/or city council would constitute the urban renewal authority. They would operate independently of the city government. In some cases, such as New Haven, the mayor used Urban Renewal as his major thrust, and kept in almost constant daily control. There were other cases, especially where there was a politically weak mayor, where he might be more a tool of the Urban Renewal Authority and subordinate to it.

Urban Renewal was the most important urban legislation ever passed because it heralded a complete change in the relationship of the Federal system: It permitted the federal government to subsidize the activities of localities. That was a revolutionary concept in this country, because the Constitution confers all powers not specifically reserved to the federal government to the states. Prior to the enactment of Urban Renewal, the overwhelming majority of

37

federal grant-in-aid programs were directed to the states, and then allocated to the cities by the state governments. But Urban Renewal was different; it created a direct financial pipeline from the federal government to the cities. It instantly created a new constituency for the federal government, the mayors, city officials, and local government people. It gave great impetus to the profession of urban planning.

The 1949 Act authorized the cities to select the areas for improvement which had to be residential slum or blighted areas, or non-residential blighted areas. Open spaces could be selected if they would become residential areas. The Act allowed the government to make three kinds of benefits available:

1. Advances for surveys and plans. These were repayable loans to institute the process of selecting the blighted areas, and for planning their redevelopment.
2. Second, long term loans of forty years would cover the cost of land. Or, temporary loans, over a period of ten years would carry the burden of salaries, fees for professional services, and expenses.
3. The main benefit would be capital grants that would cover a portion of the net cost of the development.

The 1949 Act appropriated $500 million, an astronomic amount of money in those days. Over the next quarter century Congress appropriated over $6 billion under Title I, called capital grants.

This is the formula: The net project cost is the result of adding up the acquisition, the planning and clearance costs, minus the sales price to the developer. There is always a net loss. The developer pays less than the city's cost for buying and clearing the land. This is the whole rationale for Urban Renewal. Namely, that in these blighted areas there is no private incentive to acquire or develop this land; rather, public initiative is needed to perform that role, involving acquiring, blocking up, clearing, and then making the land available at a write-down.

To the developer "write-down" was the key phrase in the Act.

In the concept of direct federal-city relations, it is inherent that the federal government would make certain requirements of the cities, since it was paying the bills. The conservative political forces have always emphasized this—that the federal government would control the expenditure of the money. Beginning in 1949, certain requirements were made:

1. The city should get the correct legal authorization from the state through the passage of an enabling act.
2. There must be an adequate plan for acquiring and developing the properties. The government had the right to review the plans to determine if they were adequate.
3. The community had to show a need for federal aid. This was a "first come, first served" program from its inception. It did not set up criteria for participation, but, in theory, was open to every locality in the United States.
4. There must be a clear intention to give maximum consideration to private enterprise. The concept was to be framed in such a way to give incentives to private development, and to remove obstacles in its path. (Public Housing took the same position in 1937—there was resistance to the public sector developing or owning.)
5. A public hearing had to be held before the land purchase.
6. A city must be financially strong enough to provide its share, or one-third of the net cost.
7. There must be a provision for the relocation of displaced families.

The next significant development of Urban Renewal was in the Act of 1954, which revised the program. The 1954 Act was largely the result of an influential Presidential committee, appointed by President Eisenhower, called the Advisory Committee on Housing. This Committee strongly recommended rehabilitation and conservation in contrast to a total reliance on clearance as an urban redevelopment tool, because criticism had already arisen about the wholesale slum clearance program.

One of the most dramatic sagas on Urban Renewal, *The Urban Villagers*, by Herbert Gans,[1] tells the story of the West End of Boston. In the Urban Renewal project there, a whole community of Italians was disrupted and a neighborhood destroyed. The question was already being asked, "Why destroy these people's homes? Why not let them remain in their neighborhood and give them some help in remodeling and conserving their neighborhood?" I took a keen personal interest in Gans' story of the Italians in Boston because I was seeing at close hand a similar disruption in the town of Milford, Connecticut. Mayor Charles Iovino had appointed me to a Citizens Advisory Committee in 1962 because I served as a student worker in a local church. The church building was located in a proposed Urban Renewal area and the city fathers wanted my help in gaining public support for the project.

I favored the Urban Renewal concept. In a seminar at Yale, I had the opportunity to examine the program closely and as a "liberal" young minister to be I thought the church should be positive in its approach to redevelopment of slum areas.

But there was the rub. The area around the church was not a *slum*. It was a coherent neighborhood of working people who had bought homes which had formerly been used by wealthy families for summer "beach houses." Many of the homes had been winterized and made into substantial dwellings. True, many of them had been allowed to run down by absentee landlords. But on the face of it, it was not logical or equitable to displace *all* the families and clear the whole neighborhood. So, the young liberal the downtown establishment wanted for support became an opponent of the project! All my arguments for a *mix* of rehabilitation and clearance fell on deaf ears. The urban planners in Milford were still living in the 1950's and unfortunately helped to sustain the image of Urban Renewal created by Martin Anderson in *The Federal Bulldozer*.

Anderson's book, which was published in 1964, and received much publicity, argued that:

> The basic premise on which the program was started . . . is that Urban Renewal eliminates slums, prevents the spread of blight, and revitalizes the cities. It is much more likely that the . . . program shifts slums instead of removing them, and, in so doing, may actually encourage the spread of slums and blight. The people who move from the Urban Renewal program are not really helped by the operation of the program.[2]

The experience of Boston's West End and other such examples led to the Committee's emphasis on rehabilitation, but there was also a financial motive in the President's Committee which was that rehabilitation would cost the government less.

To implement this new emphasis on rehabilitation, the tools had to be provided to make it possible. The first change in the FHA programs occurred as a result of Urban Renewal. City officials trying to implement Urban Renewal soon found that they needed other tools. Urban Renewal itself did not provide all the resources available to solve the problems that it discovered. So, the National Housing Act was amended by the Housing Act of 1954 to provide mortgage insurance for persons in the rehabilitation area who wanted home improvement loans. That was called Section 220.

Another new tool, Section 221, provided mortgage insurance on sales of housing for persons displaced by Urban Renewal. This was instrumental in helping a person in a total clearance situation who had no money to buy another house. He could benefit from FHA mortgage insurance.

Another significant part of the report of the Advisory Committee was that the Act of 1949 was somewhat lax in its criteria for the cities. They were broad, not specific, and they were not enforced with the strictness that the Committee desired. A significant innovation of the Act of 1954 was the introduction of the concept of a "workable program for community improvement." Local eligibility requirements were tightened, and procedures to be followed by the city were specifically outlined.

Another assumption made was that the cities had the technical capacity to fill out the applications and get Urban Renewal programs started. The assumption was incorrect since most cities did not have the experienced personnel to do it. So, the government hired more people to give federal assistance to the localities.

Most cities had no guideposts and no experience with redevelopment. Therefore, a new Urban Renewal demonstration grant program was provided to give certain cities extra money to develop, test, and report on new and improved methods of redevelopment.

The Act of 1954 set forward a significant program, still in existence, known as 701 planning. The program was available to states and cities for regional or state planning. Once the choice was made to redevelop a blighted area, the area had to be selected and specified. Then the question had to be confronted of what should the plans be for the whole city or region. The plan and redevelopment of the specific area fits into the over-all city planning. Urban planning was not a very advanced art in this country in the 1950's. It has only become whatever there is of an art today because of the institution of 701. Most city plans done in the last fifteen years probably have been partly financed by the Department of Housing and Urban Development, under Section 701 of the Housing Act of 1954.

The Housing Act of 1949 also authorized 810,000 units of public housing. It was intended by Senator Robert Taft and others that Urban Renewal would not be separate and detached from the Public Housing program, but integrally related. When houses were torn down, people displaced were guaranteed the right of first entry into the housing under the Act. A significant amount of public housing was to be built. The authors of the 1954 Act had seen that something had to be done, even if the communities were opposed in general to public housing. Congress however, was parsimonious in its appropriations. Something had to be done to put public housing in Urban Renewal areas or Urban Renewal would not succeed. A mayor might not be attentive if the proposal was just for some public housing, but would probably be receptive if a $10 million project could not go ahead unless it included some public housing. The Housing Act of 1954 authorized 35,000 public housing units specifically for communities undertaking Urban Renewal projects.

The next Act, the Housing Act of 1956, further strengthened the Urban Renewal program by allocating relocation payments for individuals, families, and businesses displaced. It is almost fantastic to think now that in the Acts of 1954 and 1956, when substantial improvements were made, that the whole burden of relocation fell on the city, with no federal financial assistance. Of course, this became impossible. The Housing Act of 1956 allocated $100 to families and individuals, and businesses could get up to $200 to cover moving expenses. Contrast this to the Uniform Relocation Act of 1969 which provides up to $15,000 for every family that must relocate because of dislocation by a federal program. The great dislocator of people is not Urban Renewal, however, but the highway program. The Uniform Relocation Act came after abuses in the highway program; Urban Renewal is second in terms of number of people dislocated.

The Act of 1956 focused on another problem which Urban Renewal revealed: the plight of the elderly. The Act of 1956 allowed new federal assistance to the elderly in public housing and in FHA mortgage programs. For instance, under section 203, which was the FHA mainline insurance program, terms were liberalized to facilitate home purchases by persons sixty or older. The Urban Renewal program was finding that there were numerous elderly people in older, blighted areas, and there should be no discrimination under the FHA programs because of age.

The 1956 Act also provided for a general neighborhood renewal program. In the 1954 Act, the requirements for localities to have a Workable Program were set forth, and Section 701 made provisions for state and regional planning agencies. It was discovered, however, that the cities themselves, at a medium scale between the neighborhoods and region, also needed a renewal planning process.

The 1956 Act also reflected some wisdom about rehabilitation. It was not enough to provide the new FHA programs, whether by clearance or rehabilitation, because strict credit requirements had to be met to qualify for those programs. It was impossible to try to renew the inner cities of America with no subsidies except the

Urban Renewal subsidy itself, which was inadequate for the individual. The really poor, the preponderant majority of the people who lived in those areas, were not helped because of the strict requirements. So in 1956 there was an increase in the amout of money that could be borrowed by an individual under FHA for home improvements from $2500 to $3500.

The Housing Act of 1961 authorized the cities themselves to purchase and remodel homes. New Haven was the first city to carry out a program under the 1961 provision. There is a beautiful project there on Court Street. Thirteen townhouses in the Italian section of New Haven were remodeled and then sold to families.

In 1961 President Kennedy set the tone for a still broader concept of Urban Renewal. He said to the 87th Congress, "Our Urban Renewal efforts must be substantially reoriented from slum clearance and slum prevention into positive programs for economic and social regeneration."

As we look back over the history of Urban Renewal, the following trends seem evident:

1. There has been a steady cognizance that slum housing is not the only problem. The development from total clearance, then rehabilitation of housing of poor people, to economic and social considerations, emphasizes this fact.
2. There has been a steady process of emphasizing planning which has not been a developed art in our country. It was stimulated basically by Urban Renewal, the Workable Program, the Neighborhood Renewal Program, and the 701 program of 1954.
3. The problem of relocation has been a constant source of major concern. First there was no assistance, then the paltry assistance in 1954 and 1956, increased assistance in 1959, and finally, ten years later, the Uniform Relocation Act which provides generous assistance. There has also been a steady strengthening of the guidelines for relocation. When I was living in Milford, Connecticut, the Urban Renewal program was in the planning stage. The planners had to provide a relocation plan as required under the act. That relocation plan was a list of all the houses which were for sale outside the Urban Renewal project and had been taken out of the newspapers. That was the extent of their relocation plan— to tell the government which houses were for sale. A relocation plan today would contain hundreds of pages, showing extensive market studies. That is how the history of relocation has evolved.
4. There has been a steady shift in the emphasis from clearance to rehabilitation and conservation.
5. The role of credit has become an indispensable adjunct to

any program, and there has been a constant liberalization of FHA insurance terms.

6. The plight of the elderly has loomed larger and larger in the plans and continues to do so.

How did cities and towns get into the Urban Renewal program? The seeds of any Urban Renewal effort lie in the voiced concern of local citizens and officials about the blight of their area—usually some association of businessmen or residents gets together, or a branch within the local government begins to bring slum conditions to the attention of the city. The idea of cleaning up the area may be advanced by journalists. In many towns across the country, however, there is no feeling that there is any problem. Concern is not automatically expressed. The local government finally has to respond and take the initiative and go to HUD and say that it needs an Urban Renewal program.

The first step was planning. The city set up the agency and received grants and advances to do the planning. In order to qualify themselves under the Workable Program, certain requirements had to be fulfilled, such as:

1. Codes and ordinances. In 1954, when the act was passed that called for the Workable Program, less than 100 cities and towns in America had housing codes. Today that number is over 5,000. The single reason for that is the Workable Program. The federal government's requirement of a housing code for Urban Renewal stimulated many cities to pass housing codes that might not have passed them otherwise.

Part of the reason for emphasizing housing codes after 1954 was the direct relationship to rehabilitation. It is not possible to have rehabilitation without a housing code. This emphasis led to the Act of 1964 which created the concentrated code enforcement program. (See Chapter IV). This program gave the same rights of eminent domain as in Urban Renewal areas. In an area in the concentrated code enforcement program, each house would be inspected for violation of code regulations. The owner would have to fix it up or have it condemned, but would have the right to borrow or possibly receive grants to remodel it. The city Urban Renewal authority in turn could get grants to put in new lights, paved streets and trees, creating neighborhood improvement, not just housing improvement. After 1964, the process of housing code passage became even greater because of the desire to get into that program. That Act set up the Section 312 program, that provided for loans at 3 percent, and the Section 115 grant program for poor people.

2. The City had to have a comprehensive community plan including a land use plan, a thoroughfare plan, a facilities plan, and a public improvements program. The only specific requirement of the Workable Program put into the Act of 1954 was a zoning ordinance. That came under the comprehensive community plan, which is the reason that Houston could never have become an Urban Renewal city had it wanted to, because it is the only large city in America without a zoning ordinance.

3. The city had to have a neighborhood analysis program which laid out the residential areas, determined the location and extent of blight. Each neighborhood was analyzed in terms of its condition and specific recommendations were made for its improvement.

4. The city had to regear its organizational structure and show its administrative competency to do Urban Renewal. This affected almost every organization in the city, including the board of education, the planning and zoning board, the public housing authority, and the local redevelopment board. All agencies had to think and coordinate in terms of Urban Renewal.

5. They had to show their financing capacity. By 1954-56, some cities began to see that they did not have the money to match the Urban Renewal monies required. This led to states enacting grant programs to the cities, New York and Connecticut among the first. As small cities were the hardest pressed, the Act of 1954 gave Urban Renewal authorities the right to distinguish between cities in terms of population; cities under 50,000 were able to receive three-fourths assistance rather than two-thirds.

6. Under the Workable Program, there had to be a relocation plan. The federal government has been expressly concerned with the problems of relocation, and stringent in its requirements, but, in many cases, the city did not follow through.

7. The Workable Program required citizen participation. It is almost impossible to overemphasize the impact of Urban Renewal in our lives, because it was Urban Renewal which committed localities to hearing citizens' grievances and desires for public improvement. President Kennedy said in 1961, "Only when the citizens of a community have participated in selecting the goals which will shape their environment can they be expected to support the actions necessary to accomplish these goals."

The Workable Program required that each city have a citizens advisory committee, made up of representatives of economic, civic, church, educational, and welfare groups in the community. Many of these groups were probably more public relations boards than neighborhood participation entities, but at least the foundation was laid for "maximum feasible participation" by residents, such as was required by the Economic Opportunity Act of 1964. More specifically, detailed requirements for local participation were made in the Model Cities Act of 1966. Urban Renewal started many of the citizens advisory committees which later functioned under the OEO and the Model Cities programs. In most cases, the same areas under Urban Renewal became Model City areas and Community action areas. I owe my own career in urban housing to the idea of the Citizens Advisory Committee. As I stated earlier, my first involvement in urban housing was as a member of the Citizens Advisory Committee on Urban Renewal in Milford, Connecticut. Because of that involvement, I wrote a paper on the National Urban Renewal program. This paper was the basis on which I was employed as the Housing Analyst at the Library of Congress in 1965. My experience at the Library and at Urban America led to an invitation by the Citizens Advisory Committee for me to come to Houston in 1967!

The Workable Program created an impact far beyond the simple requirement to get into a program and be annually renewed. It initiated the passage of ordinances and codes, altered the machineries of city governments, and focused citizen awareness and participation in government.

Like Public Housing, Urban Renewal has an image which is misleading as being only for the big cities. In reality, 60 percent of all Urban Renewal projects are in cities of under 50,000; 18 percent are in towns of less than 10,000. The word "urban" throws us off; a large amount of money goes into the big cities, but it is a small town program as well as a big city program.

An Assessment of Urban Renewal

Urban Renewal was probably the most significant legislation affecting the cities ever passed. It is comparable to the Marshall Plan in foreign policy. Such an important program, one that broke new ground, would be expected to generate controversy.

First, there were many conservatives in the country who thought that Urban Renewal was socialistic. It got the government into the business of land development. Second, they said that it was too costly, and third, that it was not constitutional.

Soon after Urban Renewal got underway, after the Housing Act of 1954, the cry went up that it invaded the individual property owner's rights protected by the Constitution. Although the Supreme Court ruled on the matter in 1900 in *Berman v. Parker*,[3] each community initiating Urban Redevelopment had to answer, and has to answer still, the attacks of those who are sure they are being denied their legal rights. After all, the program involves a public body condemning property, acquiring it with public power. A city or a state or another governmental body which acquires private property for public use does it under the power of eminent domain. The state has the power to purchase the property of an individual in accordance with the due process of law, and the Constitution specifically states that just compensation must be paid to the owner when the public acquires his property. This is the method used in our country for land acquisition for schools, highways, railroads, pipelines, military bases, fire stations; in other words, any public use. And the key question is—Is Urban Renewal a proper public use?

Now it has been judged to be a proper public use by forty-five of the fifty states, and this has been upheld by the highest courts of most of the states. The Fifth Amendment states: "No person shall be deprived of life, liberty, or property, without due process of the law, nor shall private property be taken for public use without just compensation." It is the basis upon which one would decide the question, is Urban Renewal constitutional?

Federal officials tried to make the Urban Renewal regulations conform to this Fifth Amendment by requiring that a local renewal agency pay the fair market value for the property that it acquires, based on the condition that exists at the time it is acquired. The fair market value is determined by making at least two separate independent appraisals of the property. The appraisals have to be made by recognized appraisers who are familiar with local values. In setting the value on the property an appraiser must determine the value in accordance with the practices and precedents which have been established in eminent domain proceedings in state and local courts. Definitions vary from state to state. If the property owner is not satisfied with the offer made by the Urban Renewal Authority, then he has the right to appeal to the courts. The citizen may, therefore, question the procedure of Urban Renewal as it bears on the question of just compensation. But, if he appeals to the court to strike down the right to purchase the property for Urban Renewal, then he will face the formidable obstacle that the Supreme Court, and the highest courts of thirty states and Puerto Rico, have ruled that it is a proper exercise of governmental power. *Berman v. Parker* was handed down in November 1954. Justice Douglas wrote the decision:

> Miserable and disreputable housing conditions may do more than spread disease and immorality, they may also suffocate the spirits of the people who live there to the level of cattle. They may indeed make the living an almost insufferable burden. The misery of housing may despoil a community as an open sewer may ruin a river. The concept of public welfare is broad and inclusive, the values it represents are spiritual as well as physical, aesthetic as well as monetary. It is within the power of the legislature to determine that a community should be beautiful as well as healthy; spacious as well as clean; well balanced as well as carefully controlled.

In the case of *Berman v. Parker*, the court also upheld the acquisition of sound structures within a slum or blighted area. That was a key question—and also a source of great chagrin on the part of many home owners and landlords. They might have a perfectly fine home or apartment building, but in an area which is blighted in general. They were the ones naturally to complain the loudest, and that was a specific situation in the *Berman v. Parker* case in Washington, D. C., where the landlord did not own a blighted structure. So, Justice Douglas spoke specifically to that. Sound structures in any blighted area may also be condemned and purchased.

There have been some flagrant abuses of the term "public use." Take the case of Atlanta where the Atlanta Stadium now stands. This was ruled to be a blighted area, and a stadium was put in its place. In other words, it was a fine way to get the government to pay two-thirds of the cost of the land upon which the city was building a new stadium. And there are other similar examples.

The critics who focus on the cost of redevelopment usually refer to the burden placed on local citizens, that is, the local share to renew an area, plus the waste of federal funds. Martin Anderson in the *Federal Bulldozer* argues this point. Taking his philosophical position into account, which is that of a Young Americans for Freedom leader, he felt and tried to develop some statistics showing that actual dollars spent were mammoth amounts. "Huge sums of money will be required to implement the Urban Renewal process . . . The tax payers in the United States have paid and will continue to pay a substantial share of the cost of Urban Renewal." (Pp. 137, 139) Anderson argued that the probability of private investment being stimulated was low and that therefore taxpayers would really shoulder the burden of billions spent by the federal government for Urban Renewal.

Anderson maintains that the Urban Renewal program has "actually caused a decrease in the tax revenues of most cities which have Urban Renewal projects." (P. 9. Cf. Chapter Ten, "The Tax Increase Myth.") He states that the buildings would have been built elsewhere and would have yielded higher taxes.

Urban Renewal does cost money, billions, but, contrary to Anderson, it also produces substantial increases in tax revenues to the cities. The values of the property adjacent to the former slum tend to increase. Perhaps more important, blighted areas require great outlay of funds for fire, health, police, welfare services. With the elimination of slums the cost of providing these services ordinarily goes down very sharply. To illustrate, there was a case in New Haven in 1950, where before the clearance project, costs of these municipal services was $200,000 per year; the revenue from the taxes was $105,000, with a loss of $95,000. After the renewal, the service costs went down to $100,000, and the revenue increased to $315,000, an increase of $215,000, which is a net benefit to the city of $315,000 a year.

This pattern of increased revenue and decreased service costs can be documented in countless cases which have undergone Urban Renewal. For instance, in Detroit, in the area of six Urban Renewal projects, the city collected $757,000 in taxes before redevelopment, $8,318,000 after. Anderson's book was written in 1960 which was the low point of Urban Renewal in terms of its completion. That is to say, most of the cities had only begun renewal in the mid-50's so by 1960 they were in mid-stream. Washington, D. C. had acres and acres of cleared land—nobody was getting any benefit, and therefore, the cost compared to what they were getting before was astronomical.

No doubt the argument holds that the federal government is out the money to the benefit of the localities. It is costing the federal tax payer money, and we are all federal tax payers, while it is benefitting the city in terms of more money, and therefore, hopefully, less burden on the individual property taxes.

Has Urban Renewal been the destroyer of people's homes? One can muster a fairly good argument from planners that many slum areas did not contain the highest and the best use of the land, and

49

were not good places for slum dwellers. Look at it from their own point of view—that there is a kind of reverse pattern in our country, which is that the poor, who work in the suburbs, live downtown and have to go out to the suburbs. The affluent who live in the suburbs work downtown and have to go downtown. We all pass each other on the freeways in the mornings and in the afternoons. This line of reasoning leads to the theory of dispersing the poor. The trouble is, dispersal has not worked either because of zoning, transportation and discrimination barriers. In other words, it would have been fine if Urban Renewal had provided decent, sanitary housing, within means of the dislocated. If that pledge had been honored, then the theory would have worked. The theory was fine but housing was not provided in the volume that it should have been. Scott Greer put it harshly in 1965: "At a cost of more than three billion dollars, the Urban Renewal Agency has succeeded in materially reducing the supply of low cost housing in American cities."

From another perspective, is it not true that there has been some romanticizing by Herbert Gans and Jane Jacobs of the style of life in the slums? Slum life is not romantic, and I am not sure that we want to "preserve" it, and maintain these areas. They are jungles for many of the people, not just as it appears to a middle-class outsider, but from their eyes, as well, as in Claude Brown's *Manchild in the Promised Land*. Here are some of Brown's lines about Harlem:

Heroin had been the thing in Harlem . . . , and I don't think anybody knew anyone who had kicked it . . . It was like a plague. . . .

We'd get high, and we'd solve all the problems of Harlem. When it wore off, we would just have to live with them all over again.[4]

Most persons in the slums want to escape. Blacks in America have conservative ideals about housing. There are hundreds upon hundreds of brand new townhouses built in planned developments which builders cannot sell to blacks because they do not fit their image. They want a single family house on a lot where they can tend the grass and not have somebody else do it for them. Their image of what the good life is is not the Fourth Ward in Houston, or the South Side of Chicago, or Bedford-Stuyvesant in New York. The last ten years has seen black militants come forward who have their own political axes to grind. They are the ones who spread the notions of "you leave our community alone, we will take care of it." That is self serving.

Now it is true that Gans as well as others have made a strong case for the other perspective. For instance, in an article, "Some Sources of Residential Satisfaction in an Urban Slum," Marc Fried and Peggy Gleicher point out that:

> It is quite notable that the available systematic studies of slum areas indicate a very broad working class composition in slums, ranging from highly skilled workers to the nonworking and sporadically working members of the "working class." Moreover even in our worst residential slums it is likely that only a minority of the inhabitants (although sometimes a fairly large and visible minority) are afflicted with one or another form of social pathology.[5]

Fried and Gleicher claim that the values of familiarity, stability, variety, kinship ties, and social integration are high among many so-called slum dwellers, and should prevent hasty dispossession of such people.

Take the example of New Haven. The city condemned the Oak Street area, which was the heart of New Haven. I was not there in those days, in the middle of the 50's, but by reading about it and by hearing about it, it is hard to imagine a worse area than that.[6] There were dismal characters everywhere and crime was rampant. They tore out all of that. There were no tools for remodeling, but no desire to remodel either. It was impossible, so they tore it all out. First to be built back in the area was the new headquarters for the Southern New England Telephone Company. The next was a multi-unit high-rise for the upper middle class, and then, as it continued on, they had more businesses, and the New Haven Hospital located there. In other words it had become a commercial and an upper income island in New Haven. What happened to the people who lived there before? They went out to the north side of New Haven where they created another slum.

In the early 1960's Congress began to react to this all too prevalent pattern. For example, Congressman Widnall of New Jersey was appalled that it was happening throughout the country. He said, "Let's stop this. People are being displaced and they are being relocated into slum housing, high income housing is being placed there and that is a scandal. That is a moral outrage." Widnall symbolized the reaction, and he galvanized support in the Congress to try to alter the program.

Starting in 1961, each housing act had more stringent requirements to build housing for the same people back on the tracts. There was pressure to put Public Housing on the Urban Renewal tracts. There were Pruitt Igoees before then, but more came later. This gets back to the argument of many planners that Urban Renewal land was not suitable for Public Housing. Political pressure made them put the Public Housing there. But the people who lived there, the argument might run, should have been dispersed into low density, or single family homes, housing where they would have been fulfilling their ideals and where the land would have been used properly from an *ad valorem* tax point of view. Then everybody would have been happy. But too many crosscurrents were at work. The first plan was wrong because little concern was given to the people in the blighted areas. The second plan was wrong because the poor were concentrated in high rise monstrosities. Urban Renewal sites are nearly always in the center of the cities and so we have Cabrini in Chicago and Pruitt-Igoe in St. Louis. In New Haven, criticism of Oak Street caused Urban Renewal to change its policy. In the Dixwell area Public Housing is concentrated and therefore the social problems are concentrated. Urban Renewal is not outside of the spectrum of the political forces in the country. And, it has been subject to all of these tensions.

Housing has been the source of much of Urban Renewal's difficulties. The Housing Act of 1949 was set on the beautiful premise that when we have all of these Urban Renewal areas, we would have 810,000 units of Public Housing built either in the Urban Renewal sites or off.

It is not true that in no place has low income housing been built on Urban Renewal sites. In fact, in the 1960's, a majority of the 221 (d) (3) projects, below market rent and rent supplement, were built on Urban Renewal sites. There is a trend of more and more federal housing subsidies as a result of Urban Renewal officials becoming great crusaders for more housing. The best example of this was in Boston. The Boston Renewal Authority was the packager for almost every nonprofit and limited dividend sponsor of 221 (d) (3) in the City of Boston. BRA did not just wait for a sponsor, developer, or nonprofit group to come in to the FHA to get a mortgage and build some housing on an Urban Renewal site. Ed Logue's soldiers said, "Here is a piece of land we have acquired, now let's go and find a sponsor, and let's take him over to FHA and let's work with him and bang the feds on the head until we get it." They did get it. And most of the subsidized projects in the City of Boston are on the Urban Renewal tracts. We are speaking of subsidized projects—221 (d) (3), 236, but not Public Housing. Logue and every other head of the Boston Renewal Authority has had difficulty in putting Public Housing on Urban Renewal sites. In the last five years the major tool that Urban Renewal has used in Massachusetts, New Jersey, Illinois, and Michigan has been the state housing finance agencies. They have provided the financing for Urban Renewal sites. Edward Logue himself went on to a state-oriented enterprise, the Urban Development Corporation of New York. After a phenomenal beginning—constructing over 135,000 units in 1969-73—the UDC came upon the shoals of disaster in 1974 because of the adverse impact of the federal housing moratorium and the recessionary drag on the economy. The UDC relied on "moral obligation" bonds for its financing of housing development, and when its projects began to fail, the negative "fall-out" on other states was devastating (see chapter VIII for a discussion of State housing programs).

Of course, the state housing programs involve moderate and in some cases middle income families who do not cause as much difficulty as Public Housing.

The liberal criticisms can be summed up in three arguments:

1. The Urban Renewal program subsidizes free enterprise. It is what Charles Abrams said about FHA programs, "Socialism for the rich and capitalism for the poor."
2. Redevelopment housing usually is composed of homes for the upper income.
3. Urban Renewal is a way to get rid of Negroes, and other minorities, and install white middle and upper class people in their place.

The first argument has some cogency. The re-developer who builds in a previously blighted area is the beneficiary of the "write-down." Had he bought and cleared the property, it would have cost him more money. He does not receive any money directly of course, but he does benefit from the "write-down." The common rejoinder given to this protest is simple, and goes to the figures mentioned in reference to increased property taxes.

It is also argued that the "write-down" is a part of the cost of rebuilding a better community. Advocates of Urban Renewal maintain that the great expense of preparing land for redevelopment was one of the reasons why private enterprise was so reluctant to build in slums and blighted areas. It can almost be stated as an

53

absolute—there is no private incentive to renew the slum areas of America. There had to be some incentive, and Urban Renewal provided it.

Looking at it another way there is cogency in this respect; that landlords have delayed improvements with the hope that the area in which their property is located would be bought or condemned. It is a big thing for the city to announce that it is going to have an Urban Renewal project. Some owners in that area hold on to their property—holding it and not selling it—while values rise. Would there be any Urban Renewal without this kind of system? Even though there are objections and some people benefit unfairly, and there are some abuses, it boils down to, would there be an Urban Renewal program without it? The answer is obvious. Certainly we want to curb the abuses, but we should not destroy the whole structure. We must continue to redevelop our cities and relocate the people—which is impossible without a subsidy.

The second criticism pertains to the re-use of the land in redevelopment projects. The president of the National Association of Housing and Redevelopment Officials once said, "What we are achieving all too often in Urban Renewal project areas is the construction of luxury and semi-luxury apartment developments. This result has given rise to the often heard criticism that Urban Renewal is simply replacing slums with fancy apartment buildings for those in the upper income brackets, and with some justification." Persons of this persuasion are on strong ground, for the reason that the upper income market is limited and can be quickly saturated. They do not need the help and yet they are the ones who ultimately benefit from the subsidy. The greatest need is not in that class, but those who are just above qualifying for public housing.

The third criticism has to do with the removal of Negroes. This argument is summed up by Charles Abrams. "Urban Renewal is evicting tens of thousands of poor families. Most of them are Negroes." Abrams held that because most of the Negroes were thus displaced, the poor must go into Public Housing, and that "segregation is cemented."

The examples of cities using Urban Renewal to relocate Negroes are obvious to all. It prevents us from hiding this aspect. However, the whole blame should not be placed on Urban Renewal. Urban Renewal would not cement segregation by placing Negroes in Public Housing if Negroes were given more opportunities to purchase homes and if Public Housing were not prohibited from being located in the Urban Renewal area or outside of it. It goes back to the housing, which is the crux of what must be solved in this country if the cities are to be renewed properly. We need to emphasize this, because a very live debate went on in consideration of the Housing and Community Development Act of 1974. Senator Adlai Stevenson and HUD Secretary James Lynn had a colloquy during the hearings. Senator Stevenson is, like myself, appalled that HUD could believe, as was evident in their Better Communities Act, that we could have a monumental redevelopment program with more money available to the cities than ever before for development, *and not one dime for housing construction.* What Secretary Lynn in his pristine desire wanted, was a community development act which gave money to the cities for physical redevelopment and a housing allowance program which would help fewer people than were ever helped by Public Housing and moderate income housing programs. How on earth can America's cities be renewed, how can the mayors faced with the sordid past of Urban Renewal and failures in housing expect to go forward with a community development program with no housing program? The fundamental lesson of the past twenty years of Urban Renewal is that it cannot operate without adequate housing being built. *It all boils down to the problem of housing.*

No one is opposed to cities building new office structures and new municipal structures in their cleared areas. But it must be done without sacrificing the people who once lived there. We cannot expect to cement in what exists, but to renew it requires new housing opportunities, and there cannot be housing facilities without some federal, state, and city assistance. The private sector cannot build and operate housing for poor and moderate income people without a subsidy. This is an absolute. Unless these programs exist there cannot be re-development.

Taking into account all of the difficulties and criticisms of Urban Renewal, it still stands in my mind that the concept is creative in the sense that it brings together certain fundamental American principles into a practical program. It preserves the tradition in the Constitutional requirement of local and state leadership and initiative. It vests the authority in people in the community. It requires citizen participation and provides money which only the federal government can really provide. It gives localities the incentive to participate.

In spite of the difficulties with respect to housing and Urban Renewal, is it not true that without Urban Renewal and the initiative that the program required on the part of localities and developers, that we would never have had the development of housing programs that we have had? Urban Renewal caused great pressure to be exerted for better housing. Yet Urban Renewal has not done well by housing.

We should deflect a basic antipathy on the part of planners and architects, housing officials, politicians, and the public toward the process of renewal, because the real issue is better housing and more housing for the American people.

Yet there would not have been the decrease in substandard housing except for the direct impact of Urban Renewal and code enforcement. In 1960 and 1970 the census reported many millions of housing units as substandard. There were eleven million in 1960. It was down to six million in 1970. There would have been no decrease in substandard housing except for the direct impact of Urban Renewal and code enforcement. Also important was the indirect effect of the Workable Program which created such a large number of housing codes in our cities in the 1960's. In other words, what progress we have made, even though we are not satisfied with it, has in large part been stimulated by Urban Renewal.

The burden of making Urban Renewal a more humane and a more sensitive program lies not with the federal government, but with the cities because it is now their burden to determine which areas shall be so called "Community Development" areas under the new Community Development Act of 1974. It is their business to listen to the people in the community and the development areas, to determine what project they will approve and participate in.

We have come a long way in relocation. Many millions of dollars of Community Development funds that are going to the cities will be spent for relocation. Think how this compares to the 1949 situation when relocation was hardly debated.

The structure of life in our cities is such that without community planning, without slum clearance, and some remodeling, and without some condemnation, we would never have a renewal of cities —and that we must have if our cities are to prosper. No matter what we call the program, or who the people are we ask to do it, or the structure we set up, the concern about re-development and renewal cannot be carried out with something other than the Urban Renewal process. HUD Secretary Robert Weaver once said that concern with metropolitan areas and their development cannot effectively be carried out on an ad hoc basis. It requires continuing concern and the fixing of responsibility. That is what the Urban Renewal and now the Community Development program process does; it says to the city, you set up this authority, and assume the power and the responsibility to do something about the blight in a community. It is a job which must be done.

IV. THE FEDERAL HOUSING ADMINISTRATION: FROM INSURER TO SUBSIDIZER

While the Nation's cities were receiving billions of federal dollars under the Urban Renewal program to save their deteriorated cores, the Federal Housing Administration was at the same time providing the financial stimulus to millions of middle class families to locate in the suburbs.

The Federal Housing Administration (FHA) was established in 1934 by the National Housing Act as a government insurer of private mortgages. It was the solution to the foreclosures rapidly overcoming middle class homeowners. The government would encourage private lending institutions to make risk-free loans, and the government would pay the mortgage company, or insurance company, or savings and loan, in case of default on the mortgage. From the historical perspective, the first efforts appear conservative. The buyer still had to make a large down payment, and the term was for less than twenty years. Even so, in 1934 that was a real breakthrough. It established for all time the very principle of a long payout and a smaller down payment for a home purchase. The whole history of legislation with respect to FHA is of a gradual liberalization of terms, making it less difficult to purchase a home.

The 1974 Act contains a very important title on mortgage insurance, Title III, which has increased the mortgage limit of single family homes to $45,000. It decreased the down payment required to 3 percent of the first $20,000, 5 percent of the next $10,000, and 10 percent of the remainder up to $45,000. For example, prior to this recent legislation, a $35,000 home would require a $3,000 down payment; now it requires about $1,600. This supposedly permits more houses to qualify for FHA insurance and enables more people to buy. Unfortunately, the escalation of construction costs continues to put more houses out of that range.

When it was set up, the FHA program was designed to be a viable alternative to conventional financing, which, in 1934, had become impossible because of the depression. Instead of mortgage lenders having to loan money secured only by the property itself, they could make a loan which was insured. Because the insurance factor was there, the government took the position from the beginning that the interest rate should be set by Congress, and in practice be somewhat lower than the conventional rate.[1] That meant the government was acting in an indirect way as a subsidizer to the home purchaser by granting him a lower rate because of the insurance. In 1974 the FHA rate of interest reached 9½ percent, the highest it has ever been in history. At the same time the conventional rate was 10 percent. The FHA rates, however, when they are too much out of line with conventional rates, have the effect of discouraging lenders. There have been many times, especially in 1966 and 1969, when the conventional lender was not interested in making an FHA loan, even though it is insured. It is worth more to make a conventional loan and get more yield. The FHA has traditionally prohibited discounts in practice; it means that the seller has to pay the discount to the lender. In the case of a new house, the seller is the builder, or for an old house, the owner-occupant. The discount is usually added to the price of the house.

A mortgage lender determines the yield on FHA loans or conventional loans, by calculating the term, the discounts paid at the front, and servicing costs, as well as the interest rate. In tight money periods, such as 1966, 1969, and 1974, even though the rate is lower, the yield is not great enough and lenders pull back from the FHA market. A home buyer, who wants to get an FHA loan finds that the traditional sources of those loans, the mortgage companies, are not willing to make them. That creates pressure on the Secretary to raise the rates. In fact, the Nixon Administration for some years argued with the Congress that the FHA rates should not be limited by statute, but that they should be competitive with conventional rates. In other words, the same rates would apply, and the loan would be insured so that the home buyer really would not get the benefit. The mortgage company would get the benefit.

The FHA programs are identified by the numbers of Sections of the National Housing Act.

Because FHA has functioned as a mortgage insurer, it has tended to act more like an insurance company than a housing agency. The most notorious example of its internal posture is that until the early 1950's the FHA underwriting manual contained language restricting its programs to racially exclusive neighborhoods.

But then in 1968 when Congress directed the FHA to insure mortgages on inner city residences and the foreclosure rate spurted upward, the FHA was criticized for the losses. No wonder FHA officials often have a "damned if you do, damned if you don't" perspective.

Basically the system works this way: the builder of a new house goes to his mortgage company—no individual does business with FHA. The FHA does business only with what are called "approved mortgagees," the majority of which are mortgage companies, but included are savings and loan associations, banks, or insurance companies. However, the basic partner to the FHA is the mortgage company, which functions as a warehouse. It gets investors from many sources, local and distant, and it places their money with the various real estate enterprises, a large part with the FHA system.

The builder goes to his mortgage company with plans for a $30,000 home and its subdivision, and then the mortgage company submits his plans and the location of the subdivision to the FHA. The FHA sends back an approval or a disapproval of the subdivision, with reference to its facilities such as sewer, water, gas, electricity, etc. The plans for every house have to be approved according to the FHA's *Minimum Property Standards*. The architectural section of the FHA reviews the plans. Then the package goes to the appraisal section, which checks the plans and the lot. Based on the data that they have about the area, the locality, and construction costs, they assign the house its appraised insurable value, a very important figure to the builder, because it affects the maximum FHA loan the buyer can get for the house. If it is favorable, FHA issues to the mortgagee a commitment conditional upon completion of the house, and inspection by the FHA.

In order to make the application for approval, the builder must pay up to $150 cash with the application for the FHA work just described. Then, he builds the house, calls for an inspection, goes to the mortgage company, who asks the FHA by form letter for an inspection. FHA then sends out an inspector to inspect the house. If it is completed and meets their specifications, the builder knows he can sell the house if he finds a qualified buyer under the FHA program 203 (b). When the qualified buyer is found, the builder has a permanent commitment from the FHA. With the permanent commitment in hand, the builder and the buyer go to the mortgage company, which has an FHA commitment to insure the house.

In the meantime, the buyer has had to fill out his application, and the FHA gets a credit report and analysis on that individual, for which the buyer must pay some money. Then the mortgage company goes to a lender, usually FNMA now, but in the past it could have been some insurance company, savings and loan association, or pension fund. The FHA insures the loan at this closing.

In the case of an existing house, also sold under 203 (b), the procedure is similar, but somewhat less complicated. If a homeowner wants to sell his home, but believes that it might be difficult to sell it on a conventional loan and would like to see his market expanded by having it include FHA, he goes to FHA and asks to have his house inspected to see if it qualifies for sale under one of their programs. With that in hand, the person who owns the house can tell the prospective buyer to go to the FHA or, really, to his mortgage company and apply for the loan on the house. With his loan approval, and the conditional commitment on the house by the FHA, the deal can be made as on the new house.

For twenty years, FHA was involved in a single-family home buyer enterprise. Therefore, the first multi-family programs were not very important.

Section 207 of the National Housing Act allowed eight or more units built by a developer to be insured under the same FHA rate that prevailed. This also changed the tradition of doing things because apartments could be built in the way homes are—on a long return, lower equity investment. This is now down to 10 percent, whereas it used to be more like 40 percent. Section 207 still exists at a forty year term with the FHA rate of interest.

The next significant change in the single family housing program was called 221 (d) (2), which relented somewhat from the very arduous credit rules and property standards for 203 (b). 221 (d) (2) is not subsidized; the interest rate is still the FHA rate, but it is specifically directed to moderate income families. It is very close to 221 (d) (3), dealing with moderate income multi-family housing.

In Houston in the mid-60's, on the average, only one out of twenty applicants for 203 (b) could qualify. 203 (b) had become, and still is, an essentially middle class program. It is operated very conservatively. FHA relented from that somewhat in the 221 (d) (2) program by allowing some modifications in the property standards and the credit qualifications. In regard to the 221 (d) (2) program the underwriters used the term "acceptable risk"; whereas before they required a borrower to meet the test of "acceptable credit."

Simply illustrated, if a man who makes $10,000 comes up for a 203 (b) loan and it is known that he has had a car repossessed, his request will not be approved. However, under 221 (d) (2) the same

61

man, who may have had a car repossessed three years ago, but has paid his rent on time every month since, would have been considered an acceptable risk.

The next significant step in the single family FHA business was Section 235, passed in 1968. This was the first time there were any subsidies in single family insurance. In 1969-71, the interest was at 6 to 8 percent at certain times, and the mortgage company still received 6 to 8 percent, but the individual was paying 1 percent. This was the first time that there was a strict income requirement. Since the person who would qualify under Section 235 would get the benefit of a 1 percent mortgage, he had to earn not more than 135 percent of the public housing income limit.

In this case, the procedure went as follows: The builder of a sub-division does not want to sell all of the houses under Section 235; it was not intended to be a project type program. He therefore gets commitments under 203 (b) or 221 (d) (2) for his 100 houses. With 100 conditional commitments under 203 (b), fifty prospective buyers may come forward who qualify under 203 (b). They are sent to the mortgage company and make their applications to FHA, and are approved. Fifty other prospective buyers come forward, who may not qualify under 203 (b), but would under 235, so they are sent to the mortgage company to fill out a 235 application. They send that to FHA, which comes back to the builder and changes from the conditional 203 (b) to the permanent commitment under Section 235, assuming that the buyer is qualified. At the closing it is closed as a Section 235 loan.

In the statute Congress imposed cost ceilings on Section 235. The ceiling was $15,000 in the 1968 Act. Then it went up to $18,500 for a house with three bedrooms, and $22,000 for a house with four or more bedrooms. Many 235's were foreclosed because of poor planning by the builder, aggravated by the market and inflationary spiral: With a $15,000 ceiling, such as in Dallas, the market was limited to certain families earning $5,000 or $8,000 per year, with a certain number of children in order to qualify for the program, and the particular house. These restrictions were disastrous for the builders.

Houston had one of the better experiences with the Section 235 program. One company, Suburban Homes, built on the north side of Houston basically the same houses in different subdivisions, which were advertised as FHA houses and sold under both 203 (b) and Section 235.

Maladministration ruined the Section 235 program in many

places. In over twenty cities, it is alleged that certain FHA officials were in collusion with the mortgage companies to appraise the houses at a price over their value. Families were unable economically to maintain the shoddy house. Then, at the time the mechanical parts of the house started failing, and plumbing did not work, people did not have the resources to repair it, so they left. That has been compounded by thousands of cases across the country. The worst examples were in Philadelphia, Detroit, and New York, where there were convictions, not just indictments. An entire FHA insuring office in Hempstead, New York had to be closed. That is what ruined the 235 program.

But the Nixon and Ford Administrations have completely brushed over the issue of poor management by HUD, and have attacked section 235 for its "inherent" inequity and wastefulness.

The first glimmerings of a HUD retreat from the hard line antagonism to Section 235 came in October 1975 when Secretary Hills announced a reinstatement of the Section 235 program. Such an announcement indicates that the Secretary and her advisers do not believe that the program is inherently unworkable. The reinstatement does include some revisons of the program, for example, a 5 percent interest rate rather than 1 percent and emphasis on more 'middle class' consumers. At the least, the resurrection of 235 signifies the first efforts on HUD's part since 1973 to help stimulate the construction of new units for those families priced out of the conventional market.

All in all, FHA insurance programs opened up a new vista of homeonwership for American families. As Charles Haar wrote, "Mortgage finance innovations created by the Federal Government have helped accomplish and sustain the remarkable achievements of the residential housing market. The impact of the FHA and VA mortgage is felt in every sector of the housing industry, shaping both the volume and pattern of construction."[2]

Aside from monetary policies determined by the Federal Reserve Board, the Federal Government's most direct instrument in affecting the housing market is the FHA, with its mortgage insurance programs. The Secretary of HUD can regulate the interest and thereby consumer demand; Congress can liberalize the term and downpayment requirements and thereby open the market to more families; and FHA itself can moderate its standards to qualify more families for its insurance.

The past achievements of FHA were the result of a pioneering attitude—a belief in the obligation of the Federal Government to establish patterns of housing finance which would benefit the home-buyer and set new patterns opening up opportunities for American families. The challenge ahead for FHA is to regain that pioneering attitude and not become merely a *reactor* to the conventional market conditions. Homeonwership is becoming an elusive dream for too many Americans, and FHA must use its programs and policy-setting powers to keep the dream from becoming a mirage.

V. HOUSING CODES:
THE HUMAN DIMENSION

Housing Codes: A Minimum Standard of Health and Safety

"Elysian" to the ancient Greeks conjured the dream of heavenly delight—the ultimate abode of the good. In Houston Elysian is a tawdry street in the Fifth Ward. There, ironically, one may encounter first hand the unheavenly life in a "shotgun" shack.

Between patches of linoleum in the kitchen floor are treacherous holes—providing a view to the dirt below. The lights are hanging from worn out cords and the windows are clogged with cardboard.

No American family should have to live in such a fire trap.

The objection to letting children grow up in dangerous housing lies at the root of the passage of laws to protect people from these hazards to health and safety. This conviction about decent housing motivated Houstonians to vote favorably for a minimum standards housing code in November, 1969.

Such actions have a long history in America. The pressure of immigration on our largest cities created intolerable housing conditions in the 19th Century, and "As evidence of worsening slums . . . began to command the attention of local and national leaders, Congress ordered a special investigation of urban blight in 1892."[1]

Public sentiment against bad housing conditions first took tangible shape in New York City when a survey by a citizens association in 1864 inspired the adoption of the first tenement house law three years later. Another law passed in New York City in 1879 which required windows in every room.[2]

The first modern housing code, however, was New York's Tenement House Law of 1901. It allowed the City's housing department to declare a dwelling to be a public nuisance whenever the plumbing, sewerage, drainage, lighting, or ventilation was in a condition dangerous to life or health.[3]

The human dimension of housing codes and their enforcement is the important aspect. What problems of communities and residents led to the passage of such ordinances? How do housing codes assist in the effort to upgrade neighborhoods? What are the benefits and hardships expected or experienced by citizens as a result of housing code programs? What are some of the difficulties in carrying out effective code enforcement programs? What are the conditions for successful implementation?

In addition to these questions, it is also important to inquire how the Code Enforcement Program has fared in the America's cities, for although this code program has been discontinued, cities will be carrying out similar code enforcement activities under the new Community Development Program.

In the last twenty years over five thousand municipalities have enacted housing codes—ordinances requiring minimum standards for housing facilities, maintenance, and occupancy.

Subsequent housing codes enacted by localities have sought to place a minimum standard on existing housing, below which no person should be subjected.

The minimum standard in effect represents the consensus of a community consciousness about what constitutes a decent environment. The principal purpose of a housing code is to ensure that *existing* housing does not endanger the health or safety of the occupants by: 1) the presence of inadequate sanitary, heating, or cooking facilites; 2) the lack of access to light and air; 3) the crowding of too many persons into too few rooms or too little space per dwelling unit or per room; 4) serious structural inadequacies or the *absence* of minimum standard electrical and plumbing facilities; 5) poor maintenance. Stated differently, a *housing* code guarantees to the consumer of existing housing a certain quality, just as a *building* code guarantees a quality product to the buyer of a new house.

The key distinction of a housing code, which sets it apart from construction codes, is that it affects dwellings with people in them. Construction codes regulate the *building*, housing codes regulate the *living* in houses.

The administration of housing codes raises fundamental legal and constitutional issues. The specter of private property invasion is always brought up by opponents of housing codes. But the power of the government to impose housing standards to protect public order, health, safety, and welfare has been sustained by many court decisions.[4] The Fifth Amendment, of course, affects the general enforcement of housing codes by protection against deprivation of life, liberty, or property without due process of law.

Because the administration of a housing code is dependent upon the ability to enter dwellings and evaluate them, the legal challenges have most typically been of the right to inspect.[5] A Houston City Councilman once stated that inspections under a housing code would create a "police state".

The constitutional question is whether an inspection is a "search" and therefore falls within the meaning of the prohibition against "unreasonable searches and seizures" contained in the Fourth Amendment. Until 1967 the courts had ruled that housing code inspections did not constitute a "search." In *Frank* v. *Maryland* the U.S. Supreme Court upheld warrantless inspections in a five-to-four decision. But in 1967 the court held in two cases, *Camara* v. *Municipal Court of the City and County of San Francisco* and *See* v. *City of Seattle*, that a housing inspection is an intrusion upon the privacy and security of individuals protected by the Fourth Amendment.[6] The upshot of these cases is that if an inspector is refused admission, he must obtain an inspection warrant. The occupant cannot be punished for refusing entry unless the warrant is obtained. "Probable cause" must be shown for issuance of the warrant, and *Camara* laid down some guidelines for the proper issuance of a warrant. Housing codes, therefore, which expect to be sustained must conform to the edicts of *Camara* and *See*.

But the basic power of the government to protect the health and safety of persons by enforcement of minimum standards in housing stands without question.

Housing Codes: Tools To Upgrade The Community

The second major function of a housing code is to set standards for the upgrading of existing housing. It is a function which goes beyond the predominantly negative role of requiring landlords and owners either to correct gross abuses or demolish the dwelling. After World War II it did not take long to realize that slum clearance was only a partial solution to urban blight.

It became clear that *rehabilitation* also would have to be utilized for two reasons—much of the Nation's housing stock required substantial repair, but not destruction, and many neighborhoods wanted to maintain their identity, not be "cleared" into nonexistence.[7]

As President Eisenhower's Advisory Committee on Government Housing said in 1953:

> To wipe out existing slums and *to check the spread of blight* is a major goal of our housing programs. To reach this goal we must remove houses and clear areas of our cities which are

beyond recall; *we must restore to sound condition all dwellings worth saving.* In this way we can establish as healthy neighborhoods vast areas of our cities which are now blighted or badly threatened by blight. (Emphasis added)

As a result of the Advisory Committee's report the Congress fashioned the term "Urban Renewal" in the Housing Act of 1954, which included new federal housing programs to encourage rehabilitation as well as demolition of dwellings in blighted areas.

More important, however, the Housing Act of 1954 required that communities receiving federal aid for Urban Renewal be required to have a "workable program for community improvement"—a local series of efforts to stave off urban decay. Federal housing officials made a housing code one of the required efforts. In the Housing Act of 1964 Congress stipulated a housing code as a statutory requirement for certification of a workable program.

Because of the workable program requirement many communities were inspired to enact housing ordinances. The following table from the report of the National Commission on Urban Problems documents this development.[8]

INCREASE IN HOUSING CODES

Year	Number of housing codes	Source of data
1911	1	Edith Elmer Wood
1919	6	Do.
1956	56	HHFA study
1958-59	164	NAHRO directory
1961-62	341	Do.
1962	670	URA Codes and Building Standards Branch
1964-65	498	NAHRO directory
1964	(787)	PHS survey (8 States not reported).
1968	(2,972)	Workable Program Office estimate for workable program cities only.
1968	4,904	National Commission on Urban Problems survey.

Although government policy had stressed rehabilitation since 1954, a prominent expert stated in 1965 that "the unhappy fact is that solid successes in rehabilitation have been few and far between . . . we have produced more words than deeds, more plans than product."[9]

One of the main reasons for this poor record was that the tools Congress had provided were not really effective. The FHA Section 220 program passed in 1954 to stimulate rehabilitation in urban renewal areas involved no subsidy and, therefore, could apply only to middle class families. The FHA Section 221 (d) (3) program passed in 1961 had below market interest rate features but reached only "moderate" income ($5000-$10,000) families.

The special loan and grant programs (Section 312 and 115) were applicable only to urban renewal areas and were also not funded very generously. In short, there was little help to repair houses owned or rented by the poor—the majority of whom live in blighted areas.

Apart from the lack of adequate federal programs, some emphasis has to be placed on the inherent obstacles to successful attempts by cities to use codes to help upgrade slum areas.

It has been proved that a housing code is a dead letter if slum residents cannot be *relocated* into decent housing or if they cannot *finance* the repairs necessitated under the code. No municipality is going to let its code officials throw families out in the street—and rightly so. Moreover there is no wisdom in trying to force costly repairs and even fines on those who cannot afford them or on those who are exploiting a tight housing market and have little incentive to improve their property. In a situation where no other housing opportunity is available, enforcement against the slumlord will fail. As Schorr says, "Where enforcement is pitted against the businessman's incentive to make profit, enforcement is bound to be in trouble."[10] Several of the key elements that militate against property improvement are the municipal property tax,[11] the capital gains tax,[12] the basis for calculating value in condemnation, and the depreciation allowance. The property tax increases when improvements are made. The capital gains tax leads owners to hold on to property while the land increases in value; maintenance is neglected because the improvements are secondary. Condemnation payments are often based on income, not condition. The depreciation allowance tends to limit motivation to repair; rather, the incentive is to "write off" income for six to eight years and then sell. Added to all of these obstacles, the tenant often resists code enforcement, fearing that rents will have to go up if repairs are made.

Furthermore housing code administration is usually beset by problems of inadequate staffing and low budgets. "Housing inspection still fails to appeal to the public's imagination; still fails to make really substantial impact. It appears to be a dreary program."[13]

Thus tenants will fight against code enforcement if there is no decent housing available for them or if their rent will be increased. Owners will resist if financing terms are prohibitive. Landlords will ignore or obstruct code enforcement if all the incentives are in the opposite direction. Code officials are hampered by lack of public support. As Schorr says, "In a sense, the whole system conspires against code enforcement."[14] All of which is only to make clear that effective code enforcement depends on: new housing being built; favorable financing available for repair costs; a general neighborhood renewal spirit, with incentives to offset obstacles; effective administration of enforcement programs with public and neighborhood support.

With these inherent obstacles in mind it can be understood why in 1965 Congress did enact a program to assist localities in the attempt to overcome them and change the poor record of rehabilitation—the Concentrated Code Enforcement Program. Although this code enforcement program met its demise with the moratorium, cities will be carrying out similar code enforcement activities under the Community Development Program.

The Concentrated Code Enforcement Program

The development of federal policy stressing rehabilitation reached a plateau with the Housing and Urban Development Act of 1965. This Act added Section 117 to the Housing Act of 1949— the Concentrated Code Enforcement Program (CCEP). The program was conceived along the lines of the Urban Renewal program—a blighted area is selected by the locality for special upgrading efforts.

The CCEP was designed to cope with the obstacles cities face in code enforcement. It provided:

- Grants to localities for administrative costs involved in code enforcement;

- Grants for public improvements;

- Grants for relocation expenses of those displaced by code enforcement action;

- Grants to poor homeowners for remodeling; and

- Low-interest loans to homeowners and landlords to bring property up to code standards.

Eligibility

The benefits of CCEP were available to those municipalities which have a certified workable program and have adopted a comprehensive system of codes with standards conforming to one of the nationally recognized model codes.[15]

Eligible Areas

The municipality was required to select areas for CCEP which:

- Are predominantly residential;
- Have code violations in 20 percent of the dwellings; and
- Contain conditions such that the combination of code compliance and public improvements will eliminate code violations and stop the area's decline.

In addition the municipality had to assure that persons displaced would be relocated into decent housing and that its level of expenditures for code enforcement and public improvements was satisfactory to ensure demonstrable success of the CCEP.

Benefits to Localities and Citizens under CCEP[16]

Federal grants cover two-thirds of eligible project costs for a locality over fifty thousand in population or three-fourths for those below fifty thousand. Relocation payments were fully covered by the federal government. Eligible project costs included: The costs of code administration including inspections, demolition of unsound structures, office space in the designated area, counseling to residents, and relocation services; and Rehabilitation Grants (Section 115). Grants are available to individuals or families whose income does not exceed $3,000 a year and who are owner-occupants. The amount is limited to $3,500 and may be used only for correction of code violations or incipient violations. Rehabilitation Loans (Section 312) are available for 3 percent for up to twenty years to homeowners and landlords. The two benefits may be combined if the applicant can "evidence adequate capacity to repay the loan."

The CCEP, then, was an effort to overcome administrative deficiencies and lack of favorable financing. It also sought to encourage a general neighborhood renewal by providing incentives for public improvements.

By itself CCEP could not do anything about new housing opportunities. Low and moderate income housing must be provided by public and private sponsors in other areas if adequate relocation housing is to be available.

The CCEP, as is obvious from the description, did not touch the *worst* slum areas of a locality. It aimed at *gray* areas—those neighborhoods which have declined but which have a possibility of revival if given the proper incentives. Really, the overall success depends on a wide use of all federal support programs as well as private improvements stimulated by the general renewal.

Nevertheless, it is clear that few if any cities or towns can expect to achieve a significant degree of neighborhood renewal without the kind of assistance provided under the CCEP, and this is why code enforcement activities will be a central thrust of Community Development programs.

A Look At Code Enforcement In Houston

The City of Houston enacted a housing code on December 10, 1969, after the issue was favored by 63 percent of the voters in a referendum.

It was hoped that passage and enforcement of the code would be the last step toward certification of a workable program by HUD and then participation in the CCEP. Houston never participated in the Federal CCEP; therefore, its program has been affected not only by the inherent obstacles mentioned in the preceding discussion but also by the absence of essential benefits of the CCEP. However, a partial alleviation of the situation was achieved through the use of Model Cities supplemental funds. With a grant under Model Cities the Houston Housing Code Enforcement Section was able to initiate a systematic code enforcement program in the designated Model Neighborhood, which comprises the inner city of Houston. Also the Houston Housing Development Corporation, a nonprofit organization, received a grant under the Model Cities program to assist residents in remodeling homes in the Model Neighborhood.

Methods of Inspection and Enforcement

Two methods of enforcement are employed by the Houston Housing Code Enforcement Section: systematic and individual complaints. Systematic code enforcement involves designation of certain areas and then a dwelling-by-dwelling inspection by evaluators. The objective of this approach is the improvement of entire neighborhoods by the enforcement of the housing code.

The individual complaint method simply means responding

on a complaint-by-complaint basis. When a complaint is filed with the Housing Code Section, mostly by anonymous calls, an evaluator is sent to make an inspection of the dwelling.

Systematic code enforcement is limited to the Model Neighborhood, while individual complaints received come from the entire city. Once a dwelling is inspected by either method and violations are discovered by an evaluation a series of letters is sent to the owner before the issuance of a ticket or legal action is taken.

Upon completion of the inspection a "correction letter" is sent to the owner with a form listing what violations of the code are present. The Chief of Houston Housing Code Section states that between 50 and 60 percent of the dwellings inspected are repaired shortly after receipt of the correction letter.

After three weeks, or four weeks when an extension is granted, a recheck is made of the building. If no action has been taken to correct the violations, a "final notice" is sent to the owner. The Chief reported that another 10 to 15 percent make corrections after receipt of the final notice. Within two to three weeks of sending the owner a final notice, a second recheck is made of the dwelling. If no progress has been made, an "expiration notice" is sent to the owner, followed by a third recheck. At this time if the violations are not corrected the owner is ticketed and legal action follows. The general time lapse from the initial inspection to final ticketing of the dwelling is three to four months.

Unoccupied structures, where violations exist, may be placarded immediately upon inspection and the dwelling may not be used until repairs are made. If an owner cannot be located or an owner refuses to repair or rehabilitate the dwelling, the Housing Code Section can have all utilities disconnected and the dwelling demolished and assess the demolition costs against the property.

The grant from Model Cities provided $250,000 for demolition of abandoned structures. Until the funds were made available, demolition could take from six months to a year or longer.

An Evaluation

Once a team of evaluators is assigned to an area and has operated within that area for a period of days, the neighborhood soon begins to recognize the officials. This establishes a sense of community responsiveness to the idea of upgrading the neighborhood. When given an area, the evaluators begin to identify with that area and take pride in seeing that it is improved through their efforts.

In Houston the evaluators are given flexibility to work with owners to correct violations. If one owner has a number of multi-family dwellings in the evaluator's area, the evaluator can extend time to the owner to complete corrections. This flexibility by the evaluator gives him a tool to help establish good relations within the community, but if an owner does not cooperate, the evaluator has the power to ticket. The flexible tool of extensions helps the entire program in creating the feeling that the program is not repressive but is a help and benefit to the neighborhood.

Systematic housing code enforcement works most effectively in those areas whch are beginning to decline. In deteriorated areas code enforcement can only protect the inhabitants from safety and health hazards. Generally speaking, from a first hand viewing of systematic code enforcement in Houston, it appears that this is the method to be employed to salvage deteriorating neighborhoods. Of course, this confirms the policy behind the CCEP's emphasis on "gray" areas.

Right to Appeal

Once an inspection has been made of a dwelling and an evaluator has made his determination that violations exist, an owner has the right to appeal that decision. The Houston Housing Code sets up the body to handle appeals, procedures for appeal, and the ground for appeal.

The Housing Board of Appeals consists of seven members, appointed by the Mayor with the approval of the City Council. Also, the Housing Board of Appeals ". . . shall be composed in part of a member or members who are either tenants or residents of a low-income housing area or otherwise familiar with the situation of tenants and residents in low-income areas of Houston."

The Code allows an appeal from an evaluator's decision on the basis of hardship. However, in all cases in which hardship is claimed, the board rather than the evaluator has the authority to waive compliances. "All cases in which hardship is claimed shall be submitted for written decision of the Housing Board of Appeals, whose determinations shall be based on the risks to health or safety weighed against the financial distress and hardship involved."

Whenever the appellant of the Housing Code Enforcement official is aggrieved by a decision of the Housing Board of Appeals, either party may make a written appeal to the City Council.

A brief summary of two of the cases before the Appeals Board exemplifies the "human" dimension which is central to housing code enforcement.

1) A widow and her grown son live in a house with no lavatory in the bathroom; no electric plugs; no electric light switches; bad flooring; improper vent on the water heater; porch coming away from the house; wall paper hanging down in different rooms of the house.

The lady and her son, who has had both legs amputated, earn $50 per week plus $10-$12 for renting out a room.

The Appeals Board decides to require the lady to repair the floor and porch within one year, to install a lavatory within one year, wall plugs within sixty days, light switches within ninety days, and to remove the hanging wall paper within thirty days. A Board member also referred her to the Houston Housing Development Corporation for financial assistance for the repairs.

2) A landlord owns an apartment house adjacent to an area being purchased by a large corporation. He does not want to make any repairs pending a sale. The evaluator cited rats, roaches, no paint, only two bathrooms for five apartments, and drainage from a washing machine into the street.

The Board stated that the landlord must vacate and demolish the building, and that it would not grant any relief.

The first case shows evidence of restraint and helpfulness which is commendable, while the second shows a firmness entirely warranted.

Each case which comes before the Board is unique, and the whole community is benefiting from wise and fair consideration on the part of the Board.

Conclusion

Houston, through the Model Cities grant, has some of the aids for administration similar to CCEP, yet it also lacks many of CCEP's advantages, for example, Section 115 grants for rehabilitation. Although the Houston experience has been favorable, it confirms that only with the full panoply of weapons available under CCEP and now the Community Development Program can a city have a truly successful code enforcement program.

A Personal Note

I mentioned that Houston enacted a housing code in 1969. It

was the last major city without an ordinance setting minimum standards for housing conditions.

Passing the housing code was not easy. In the end a public referendum was necessary because the City Council would not act without it. Pressures against the passage of the code were strongly expressed to the Councilmen in public, but more so in private.

Frankly those of us on the Mayor's Citizens Advisory Committee on Housing who drafted the code were surprised at first at the opposition. Mayor Louie Welch said on the day the code was presented to City Council that it would be "noncontroversial." None of us believed that srong exception could be taken to such a basic requirement for urban living.

Yet we were wrong. There is still that segment of our society which bristles at the slightest hint of additional governmental authority. In part it's a healthy concern about the expanded and expansive role of public power in our daily lives. But it also can become the expression of prejudices by the privileged against those most likely to benefit from the expanded authority, namely the poor slum dwellers. It was instructive to us that those who were prospering from the status quo were the strident complainers that a housing code would invade property rights and create a "police state" in Houston.

The opponents also reflected a typically Southern and perhaps Southwestern animus against federal involvement in urban affairs. Inevitably many citizens thought that the real reason for wanting a housing code was to qualify for federal programs. Much of the debate in Houston, therefore, focused not on the merits of a housing code but on the federal housing and urban renewal programs in other cities. We spent a large amount of time discussing New York's housing difficulties rather than Houston's need for a code. Again, the opponents had sniffed out a part of the truth. It's doubtful that we would have pressed so hard for the code without having in the background the hope of getting more federal money into Houston for new housing, code enforcement, and public improvements.

The whole issue of whether the Mayor and the Committee really wanted the code only to qualify for federal money came to bear on the city's entry into the Model Cities program.

When I appeared before Council in April 1968 to present the application for a Model Cities planning grant I told them that a housing code was not legally required for participation in Model

Cities. However, as the next chapter will show, HUD later extracted a promise from the Mayor that Houston would in fact pass a code if it were to receive Model Cities funds. So several Councilmen accused us of a "double-cross." In short, they could accept the Model Cities money but not a housing code.

By October 1969 Mayor Welch determined that the only way to get a housing code passed was to have a public referendum.

The strategy of the campaign was to mobilize the intended beneficiaries of the code—the residents of run down housing—and the broad spectrum of the citizenry which had a stake in a city which was eradicating slums and making life healthier. This strategy isolated the slum lords and the lower-middle class opponents of "Federal Control." The winning combination was a coalition of the poor, mostly minority, neighborhoods, and the affluent, mostly white, section of Houston. It was effective and the referendum was passed by 63 percent of the voters.

Fortunately, by loading the housing code question with the issue of other federal housing programs, the referendum took on the appearance of approval of Houston's general thrust for more and better housing for the poor. In the aftermath of the victory, it became considerably less difficult to pursue the other objectives of the Citizens' Advisory Committee—to obtain a Workable Program, to stimulate the construction of lower income housing developments, to rehabilitate blighted homes in the inner city. Looking back, the referendum which we all dreaded redounded to the benefit of many poorly housed Houstonians. The long months of controversy and political maneuvering were worth the effort!

'There's a roof over your head—if you don't lean too heavy on the walls'

'Far be it from us to interfere with your way of life'

We Gotta Be Careful . . . Indoor Plumbing Might
Be Unconstitutional

VI. MODEL CITIES: CAPSTONE OF THE GREAT SOCIETY

In the 1960's planners and government officials, especially on the local level, complained about the myriad of programs in the Federal categorical grant system—a system of hundreds of programs each requiring a different application process for a locality, each program administered by a different agency of the government. When I was working for the Congress in 1965 I would often write in speeches that there were 112 different grant programs which the mayor of a city had to learn before he could get all of the things which he needed to help his city. Of course, the number kept growing; it got up to 400 or 500 by the end of the 1960's.

It was this continual burgeoning of programs that led people to argue that there ought to be some coordination and concentration of federal programs on behalf of the cities.

From the local perspective it was felt there should be more local planning, more flexibility, more local initiative, and less federal interference. Those themes came to their most tangible expression with the Demonstration Cities and Metropolitan Development Act of 1966. The principal author of the Act was Robert C. Wood, the Under Secretary of HUD to Secretary Weaver, and formerly a professor of political science at M.I.T. He is now a university president. His academic pursuits had enlightened him about the local situation. He wrote a book entitled *1400 Governments*, illustrating the fragmented governmental responsibility in the New York City area. Before going to HUD he chaired a task force which conceived a plan to allow the localities to go into the federal "supermarket" and take all of the programs that they would need for their local area, but under a new process it would be done in a coordinated fashion such that the programs would all be concentrated in one area geographically, and would be run from one administrative source, making the impact much greater. From the federal level the approach had the appeal of the federal government getting more bang out of each buck. Instead of having cities shopping for each of these different programs, for health, education, transportation, etc., in a separate and fragmented way, they would coordinate these programs into a unified approach.

This approach was the hallmark of the Model Cities Program. It was called "Demonstration Cities." When the HUD people went over to meet with President Johnson to get his approval so that they could go forward, he said, "Look, this is 1965, and we don't want any demonstrations in the cities!" He wanted to call it something else. Thus the name Model Cities was born. The Act is named Demonstration Cities, but they could not call it "demonstration" cities because it might conjure up an image of the demonstrators in the streets.

The Model Cities concept was to coordinate and concentrate— that was the key concept at both the federal and local level. The federal government would allow the localities selected, the "Model Cities," to take a specific area in their city, an area which had the most poverty, the worst housing, the least education. Into that area, instead of having each and every program involving education, health, and welfare coming to it through a separate channel, the federal government itself would set up a program which would flow into the cities through one channel. And this locality which had previously been required to apply separately for each of the federal projects would still have to apply legally to those agencies who were authorized to disburse the monies, but the funds would all flow through this channel of Model Cities. A federal Inter-agency Committee was set up in each region so that all the applications could be reviewed in a co-ordinated fashion. The carrot for the city to do this was a pot of money additional to the already existing federal programs. The Model Cities program provided an additional cash grant, a 100 percent non-matchable grant. In coordination with the existing programs, new programs could be funded with a Model Cities grant. The typical local planner's thinking might go like this: the hospital program is not tailored to our needs; we need smaller neighborhood out-patient clinics, which the federal government under its present categorical program will not support. So why don't we use the Hill-Burton hospital facility in connection with a neighborhood out-patient clinic? Since the Hill-Burton hospital program is the normal hospital program it will finance one aspect of the program, but this additional cash grant from Model Cities will support the out-patient clinic.

The second use of that money, which was considered crucial, was as matching funds for other federal programs. Most of these other programs which had been passed since the War were matching programs. For example, the Hill-Burton program for construction of hospitals required a 50 percent match by the non-federal sponsor. The Educational Facilities Act required colleges or secondary schools to match those monies. With Urban Renewal a locality had to put up a third to get the program. They had to prove that they could pay that much money. It was argued that some cities were not utilizing these programs because they could not afford that match. So, in addition to using the monies from Model Cities for new programs, which were locally planned and locally directed, they received money to match other federal programs. The cities which were selected for the Model Cities program had an advantage over others because they would have a way to match all of the programs. By this method the Congress led the federal agencies to place emphasis on the towns or cities that were selected as Model Cities because they had the financial capacity to match the federal categorical programs.

So much for the overall concept. The law set up a completely different system of selection from that of Urban Renewal. Instead of a "first come, first served" legal entry, the law specifically stated that the Secretary of HUD could select the cities and that there would be a process by which he would receive applications —he would award some and deny others. Naturally, if every city in the country had been in the program it would have required untold billions of dollars. But there was not that much money. Congress authorized on the order of $500 million each year for five years. It was intended that there would be one year of planning and five years of action under the Model Cities program. There were to be two rounds of selection. There were "first round" cities and "second round" cities. Some were chosen in 1967, and some in 1968.

Model Cities was capstone of the "Great Society." It assumed the viability of all the federal grant-in-aid programs. In other words, it did not challenge that system. It tried to make better use of it. In the minds of the authors of the Act as well as the Congress it was certain that the cities which had made the most use of the categorical programs, such as Urban Renewal, Community Action, and highway construction would be the ones to get into Model Cities programs. There was a certain arrogance on the part of the cities which were involved in all of these things that this was their program. That was an almost fatal flaw politically. How is it possible to get a majority of 535 Congressmen and Senators, most of whom are from small towns, to vote for a big city bill which was certainly known as a "gild the ghetto" measure? It was an "LBJ gild the ghetto" measure—a complete turnaround from the notion of dispersal of people from the ghetto. The Rent Supplement program was sold in 1965 on the basis of being a housing dispersal tool. Within that year, 1965-66, New York, Philadelphia, and a lot of other places burned, and many spokesmen urged the federal government to build up the ghetto. Model Cities in 1966 was riding the crest of that wave. Model Cities money was to be concentrated right in the central cities of America.

It was historically on target, but could it pass Congress? President Johnson solved that—he went to a Senator from a small rural state, Edmund Muskie, and said, "You don't have an ax to grind, you don't have any big cities in your state, and yet you are very interested in inter-governmental cooperation." Muskie was the Chairman of the Intergovernmental Relations Subcommittee of the Governmental Operations Committee, and still is. This Committee had published studies about inter-governmental relations in the federal system. Muskie said he would help if certain changes were made. The first change was that every state must have at least one Model City—even Montana, Idaho, and Maine, in other' words. He wanted a certain percentage of funds to be spent in small towns. That toned down the big city image. Subsequently Muskie did a masterful job of shepherding the bill through the Senate.

Model Cities appealed to Congressmen who wanted to tighten up the programs and wanted to contain the pressure throughout the country to do something about the problems of the ghetto.

The Houston Story

For Houston, Model Cities was a briar patch. Not too many people in Washington guessed that Houston would be interested in it. First, it was a culmination of the federal grant-in-aid process. It was assumed that the cities which had participated like New Haven, Philadelphia, New York, and Boston, would be the main ones to get into the program. Of course, they did. But here was Houston which had never been in Urban Renewal. It was assumed that Model Cities would build on Urban Renewal. But it was widely assumed that Urban Renewal had not responded appropriately to the social dimensions of urban problems, so Model Cities was to be very socially oriented—software projects could be funded as well as physical development. Model Cities

83

responded to the criticisms of dislocation, and the law itself was much more stringent than Urban Renewal ever was regarding relocation. At least 40 to 50 percent of the money in the ghetto was actually spent on relocation, especially in the bigger cities. It responded to the Community Action principle of resident participation more strongly than Urban Renewal ever did and required a strong and genuine citizen input. It did not specify how citizen participation should be implemented, but it required the city to show HUD how the citizens would be involved. It was a culmination of the "Great Society" temper.

Houston had not participated in Urban Renewal, concentrated code enforcement, and had not even built any public housing in nearly twenty years. Why was there interest in Model Cities in the first place? There was interest in it because of some historical quirks. Since Urban Renewal required a Workable Program, which in turn required a zoning ordinance and other codes and ordinances, Houston had never been able to qualify because it did not have a zoning ordinance.

When Lyndon Johnson became the Vice-President, he persuaded Housing Administrator Robert Weaver to approve Houston's Workable Program. He gave Houston a Workable Program in 1961, but even at the urging of the Vice President he could not flout administrative regulations, so the approval of the Workable Program was given on the condition that Houston enact a zoning ordinance. In 1962, one year later, there was a referendum in Houston on whether to enact a zoning ordinance and it was defeated, as it had been several times before. Houston's Workable Program lapsed—it was not re-certified. Because Houston did not have a Workable Program, it could not have participated in Urban Renewal even if it had wanted to; it could not have any new Public Housing if it had wanted it; and it could not build 221 (d) (3) below-market-rate interest housing either.

The authors of the Model Cities program omitted any reference to a Workable Program. They let the largest urban program conceived up to that time slip by without putting in what to HUD was almost a religious article—the Workable Program. The Workable Program served as a ticket to get into the HUD supermarket. Some communities certainly used the Workable Program in a manner opposite to the intentions of Congress. They decided they did not want the ticket. Do not ask for the ticket and you don't have to participate in Urban Renewal, public housing, or code enforcement. This line of reasoning was used in Houston. There were some persons who did not want to make the effort to get a Workable Program because they did not want the things it brought.

Model Cities emphasized local control. It was often said that there was not going to be a manual as there was with Urban Renewal. "Red tape" was a big specter which the Model Cities Program was supposed to reduce.

The reason that the authors of Model Cities overlooked putting in the requirement for a Workable Program in the Act was that they thought that only cities with Urban Renewal would apply, and therefore, they would already have the Workable Program. But it opened the path to Houston because Houston did not have to have the Workable Program. In Houston, the Mayor's Citizens Advisory Committee on Housing was looking for ways to improve housing conditions. In 1967 right after the Model Cities act had passed, the Committee began looking into all the possible ways of getting help for Houston's poor housing. The Committee saw that Model Cities did not even require a housing code which had been proposed in Houston but which had not yet passed. It did not get passed until 1969, as was mentioned in Chapter IV.

So there was no legal impediment in the way of Houston's applying. Among the big cities applying, Houston was the only one which had not been in the Urban Renewal Program.

The application process was interesting. Because the assumption was still strong that only Urban Renewal cities would apply, HUD's response to Houston's application was at first incredulous. The feedback from the grapevine was, if you do not have Urban Renewal, how do you expect to get into this program? Houston's leaders argued that Urban Renewal was not appropriate in the city. Land could still be acquired in large quantities and at reasonable prices. (This argument was proven correct in 1969 when Texas Eastern Gas Transmission Company acquired thirty-two downtown blocks for development.)

Houston was a second round applicant in 1968. HUD dribbled out the announcements of the selected cities. In October they announced fifty cities had been awarded, and then on November 15, they announced eighteen more, making sixty-eight. Then a few weeks later they announced six more, that was seventy-four, and still Houston was not one of them.

The Citizens Advisory Committee on Housing was comprised of about eighty persons whose interest was in stimulating housing improvement. The Committee was to do five or six different things—set up a housing development corporation, pass a housing code, get the workable program, and finally, secure a Model Cities Grant. A special task force on Model Cities was organized to prepare the application to HUD. The whole Committee and the Mayor had to put their stamp of approval on it before it went to the City Council, which, reluctantly, approved it. Of no small importance was a letter to Mayor Louie Welch from the Governor of Texas, John Connally—which arrived the day of the presentation of the Model Cities application to the Council. I had asked an executive assistant in Governor Connally's Office for the help—knowing the conservative Council members would be influenced by Connally's endorsement. The letter said,

> I believe that this particular federal program holds promise as a prototype for a more flexible approach to federal grants-in-aid. This will certainly be the case if cities with innovative leadership, such as Houston's, participate and strongly press for local flexibility to meet diverse needs.

(Perhaps this is a minor skeleton in Republican Connally's past!)

The Council also acted partly because Martin Luther King, Jr. was assassinated two days before the vote was taken. King's death assured the passage. That was April 10, 1968.

In December of 1968 the word was out in Washington that only seventy-four cities were going to be awarded in the Model City Grants second round. Seventy-five had been awarded in the first round. It was apparent that HUD was going to deny Houston's entry into the program. In fact, on about December 1st, a letter had been received from the Ft. Worth Regional Office of HUD to the Mayor denying the application, but it had come about three days after I had made connection with an architect on the committee, Harry Golemon. Golemon had a friend, Bill Stinson, who happened to have just come from working in the White House. We told Stinson that it looked like we were not going to get a Model Cities Grant. He said, "Well, I'll see what I can do." Two days later Blair Justice from the Mayor's Office and I were in Stinson's office in Washington. We all got on the phone to a top assistant to the President, Larry Temple. The question posed was, why had Houston not been named? Temple said he would find out. We hung up and we waited anxiously two or three more hours. The telephone call came back and Temple said Robert Wood had been called by Joseph Califano, chief domestic aide to LBJ, and Wood said Houston is not going to be in because it does not have zoning.

Doesn't have zoning! Should we laugh—or cry—or get angry? What was he saying? That Houston should not have applied in the first place? But we had been encouraged by the top Model Cities official, Ralph Taylor, to apply. Was it because we could not carry out Model Cities without zoning and Urban Renewal? But Taylor and a few others in HUD had claimed that "innovative" methods of redevelopment were to be stressed.

It was certain that our civic pride was hurt. We were the sixth largest city in America, and the fact that the absence of zoning or urban renewal should be grounds for denying the poor families of our blighted areas a chance to benefit from a new and hopeful federal assistance program seemed unfair. Besides, our leaders had taken on some risks just to suggest that Houston participate in the Model Cities program. How galling to be told we were not acceptable!

We could not sit still with Wood's answer. Through Stinson, Temple arranged a meeting between Mayor Welch and President Johnson. The President welcomed the Mayor as a man who had "beaten the Establishment" in Houston to get elected. In LBJ's eyes Welch was a spokesman for the underpriviliged in Houston. So, LBJ implied, why is the Government hesitating to help the Mayor and the poor citizens of Houston (Texas' largest city!).

Welch explained that the lack of zoning should be no legal impediment. Califano had done some research after the Wood reply and backed up the Mayor. But then Califano brought up another fly in the ointment (no doubt supplied by Wood)—Houston does not even have a housing code, so how could it expect to clean up its slums? The Mayor shot back immediately that a code would soon be passed. He promised that. And with that promise LBJ turned to Califano and said, "Give Houston a Model Cities grant."

So Houston was the seventy-fifth city. This was December 1968. Nineteen sixty-nine was to be the planning year, and 1970, 1971, 1972, 1973, and 1974 were to be the action years. The grant to the city was calculated on a complicated formula of how much federal money had been coming to the city in the past. This is one reason HUD wanted to keep cities like Houston out because they did not have what was called a "base." The amount of money appropriated to Houston for each action year was about $13 million. That was the 100 percent cash grant. The program was worth about $40 million to Houston over four years. The Model Cities Program also brought millions of dollars from the other federal categorical programs.

Model Cities is no longer in existence. It has been superseded by Community Development. Another political battle during the past three years of debate about the Community Development Act was whether to include Model Cities under Community Development. There was some resistance to folding Model Cities into Community Development. Naturally the people who ran the Model Cities programs, and the people who participated in them, did not want the program to be swallowed up—they wanted it to remain a specific entity. But the HUD spokesmen prevailed because they threatened to hold back funds for Model Cities even if it were continued by Congress. The Model Cities Directors' Association, the League of Cities, and others, caved in to HUD and agreed that Model Cities would be folded into Community Development. Now the question being asked in the city halls all over America, as it is with Urban Renewal, is, what do we do with Model Cities? Just as with Urban Renewal, the people who are participating in the Model Cities programs say, "Look, give us a lease on life, let us exist just like we have been." This will not be the case in many places. Community Development funds go straight from the federal government to the city hall, not to the people. There are no stringent requirements for citizen participation. The people who are now in the city halls do not believe that "citizen participation" has been all that great. In Houston and in many other cities a certain turmoil is being generated by those who have been participating in the Model Cities. They want to know how they are going to fare under Community Development. It is inevitable, just like it was with Urban Renewal, that many of the successful projects under Model Cities will have to be continued under Community Development because they make sense. Some examples: neighborhood health clinics, social centers, street lighting, and rodent control.

Citizens who have had ten or so years of experience and participation are bound to make their voices heard. They are the people who have risen up and become spokesmen for their neighbors. They are the ones who are demanding a piece of the action. And when the Community Development areas are selected these citizens are going to play a role.

In short, Model Cities has had a great influence on how city government operates in this country. Only 150 cities participated

88

but most of the important cities of America were involved. It was ironic when LBJ had some HUD officials come to the White House to talk about the legislation and said, "I want this program to go to the mayors," because in 1966 he was already getting a lot of flack from Daley and others about the OEO program. The OEO funds did not have to go through city hall. The mayors were up in arms over it. They were saying that the OEO people were running around their cities and the mayors did not even know what they were doing. Mayor Welch in Houston was quite upset at times, especially with what the VISTA's were doing in Houston. Not that he should have had control over them, but that he thought he should, and wanted to because it was bothering him. The VISTA workers were protesting government actions and registering people to vote——people who were not likely to vote for him. That kind of thing worries a mayor. A former Model Cities Director in New Orleans, James R. King, has described the context of the situation the mayors faced:

> The strategy of the poverty program was to restore political accountability by moving from inside the White House at the federal level and from the outside at the local level. Community Action Agencies were formed as nonprofit groups to mobilize the poor against federal, state, and local bureaucrats. The first reaction of elected officials at state and local levels was one of complete horror. The federal government had officially formed a political alliance with local interests who were apparently out to do them in. At that point in time no one at any level seemed to perceive that elected officials at state and local levels, OEO, Congress, the president, and the newly formed local paragovernments had a very common problem —political accountability for a runaway bureaucracy.
> . . . The bright young men of OEO found the backing of the president and Congress was not sufficient to move line agencies into a position of political accountability. Neither did the organized introduction of citizen participation in open and heated confrontation with program professionals have anything more than a temporary and cathartic effect. The missing link for political accountability, of course, was elected officials at state and local levels. Model Cities sought to be this link.

Of course, LBJ got that message and that is why he said he wanted the program to go to the mayors, to the city government. I will never forget the crucial moment in the Houston city council presentation when the city councilmen wanted to know what was their role—how were they going to control the Model Cities program. I had to change the organizational structure, by adding a line that showed the Mayor and City Council tied to the Model City Department. The Councilmen wanted that line drawn from them down to the Model City department. So we went to the blackboard and drew that line from the City Council to the Model Cities Department. The Councilmen probably did not know what they were getting into by these actions, because once they got into control and once they had the last word, they opened the floodgates to the people who were interested in the program as workers or as recipients. In the last four years, every project that has had any problems has shown up at the city council. If a homeowner does not like the way the paint comes out on his remodeled home, he might show up at Council to protest that the Model City funds he borrowed were misused. The administrator of the project has to tell the councilmen the details about this little house; how it got painted and why the contractor ran off with the owner because they eloped and got married and the work was three months late! I had to explain such a case to them! It was not a very important case, but the point is that the City got itself involved in something which it did not bargain for in the first place. The Councilmen got educated, and many people in the neighborhoods found out about city hall and what they could do and what they could not do. The citizens did not run over the Council—a lot of persons have not got what they wanted. But city government in Houston and in other cities has changed as a result of it. Although there were wide variations, King's conclusion is valid:

> A few mayors . . . preceived this opportunity to use . . . the supplemental funds at his disposal as leverage for bringing political accountability to their own departments and to independent city agencies, which had established since the days of the New Deal, very tight and regular relationships with their counterpart providers at the federal level. They joined in the struggle for political accountability and worked with HUD generalists in the Model Cities Administration to impact on all the service-delivery systems of the federal government.

Model Cities has had an impact—an impact so deep that planners now involved in Community Development possess a certain amount of education which will affect what they are going to plan. No small measure of this education of what citizens expect of their city and its planners is attributable to the Model Cities Program.

VII. GENERAL REVENUE SHARING:
SHARING MONEY AND POWER

General Revenue Sharing has had a long history. It culminated with great fanfare on October 20, 1972 when President Nixon signed the law in Philadelphia at Independence Hall. At that moment a five-year process began of disbursing billions of dollars to local and state governments on an automatic basis. It was a breakthrough. It was a basic change in the way that the federal government disburses its funds to other bodies of government, namely, automatic payments. President Nixon, of course, claimed credit for the concept and its enactment.

But the history of Revenue Sharing is very interesting. First, the notion of revenue sharing indicates that somebody has some revenue to share. The idea of "sharing" came about in 1964. The United States was in the midst of a sustained and vigorous economic recovery. It was a year that the President's chief economic advisor, Walter Heller, took the position that the government had surplus revenue and that some of the federal money should be returned to the cities and states. This came about because of the stimulation of the economy in 1961, 1962, and 1963, a stimulant created in part by the programs instituted by the Kennedy Administration, many of which now look old in style but which at that moment were completely new and innovative. For example, under the Kennedy Administration in 1961 the Area Redevelopment Act was passed. It had been around in Congress for about five years. It was a plan to give counties and states special funds for public works so that they could build sewer and water systems, dam rivers, and construct highways to stimulate economic development and recovery in those depressed areas. That program put millions of dollars into the economy.

Another program was the public employment program which was passed in 1961. When Kennedy took office the unemployment rate was over 6 percent; by 1962 it had gone down to about 4½ percent. By 1964, the economy was moving. At the Library of Congress we wrote speeches for Congressmen saying that the United States was in the thirty-sixth month, the thirty-seventh month of a steady upward growth. In this context Heller persuaded President Kennedy and later President Johnson that a tax cut would be a particularly good economic move at that time. It would put more money in the consumer's pockets to keep up the growth. The government was already receiving more revenue because of the vigorous economy. So a tax cut was enacted in 1964. Then in the summer of 1964, Heller came out with a proposal to give block grants, or revenue, back to the cities and states. It would be a sharing of the surplus which had been generated by the growth in the economy. As a matter of fact, at the 1964 Democratic Convention, Revenue Sharing was a plank in the platform of the Democratic Party.

The plan was immediately short circuited by the war in Viet Nam. Federal expenditures in 1965 and 1966 increased. The big issue in the country, economically, politically, and philosophically, was guns or butter? In January 1966, when President Johnson made his State of the Union address, the question was, "How will the federal government pay for a stepped-up war?" Revenue Sharing was put on the back burner. It just was not viable at the time when war expenditures were increasing. Heller and the President began to speak of a "peace dividend" that would accrue in 1967. At the end of the War the United Staes would have a "peace dividend" and that would be revenue sharing. Of course that did not happen, and Johnson left office with the concept put aside.

In 1966 and 1967 Senator Jacob Javits and Governor Nelson Rockefeller focused attention on Revenue Sharing. The concept was now part of another philosophy rather than the policy of sharing revenue by the federal government. This philosophy stressed the enhancement and strengthening of the federal system. Governor Rockefeller had delivered a series of lectures in 1962 at Harvard which were published in a book called *The Future of Federalism*. Governor Rockefeller was carving out a plan for the campaign of 1964, and his philosophy was that more power, more control should be returned to the states and to the localities. He and others thought the way do do that was to try as hard as possible to eradicate the categorical grant-in-aid approach which was fragmented and dependent upon who has the best grantsmanship, who has the best planners, who can go and get money, and leaves out states and cities which do not have that expertise, but have the need.

Senator Javits was also attuned to that, and he started in 1966 and 1967 introducing bills that would implement and establish a Revenue Sharing concept. The revenue sharing concept had turned from a sharing of the surplus to a change in the system.

With this background the Nixon Administration began to advocate the "New Federalism." The major item in that program was general revenue sharing. However, by the time Nixon started advocating revenue sharing, and by the time it was actually enacted, in 1972, the deficit in the federal government had grown to its largest in history. In the last three years of the Nixon Administration, the federal deficit was greater than it ever was in the Johnson and Kennedy Administrations. The idea of revenue sharing was conceived in 1964 when the federal government actually had a surplus in the budget, but when the law was passed, the United States had the greatest deficit in its history. Nixon could rationalize that anomaly because he did not actually have in mind a sharing of the federal surplus. He wanted to return power to local government from the federal government. What he did not say, but what has now come to be seen clearly is that he did not have in mind increasing the amount of money available to the states and cities because at the same time he was advocating revenue sharing, his Administration was drastically cutting back on all the federal grant-in-aid programs. No mayor and no governor ever thought in his wildest dream that Revenue Sharing would eliminate the grant-in-aid programs. They thought it was an additional surplus, a bonus, over what they were getting. However, the "bonus" to the cities and states has come at the price of less money from the federal government for other programs. Even though revenue sharing is now a reality many other programs had been cut out benefiting cities, such as sewer grants and highway funds. This is the best evidence for the opinion that the Nixon Administration did not have revenue sharing passed on the basis of more money, but on the basis of the federal government getting out of the business of assistance to the cities and the states in the first place.

Certain themes run through the advocacy of the revenue sharing program. The primary one is that the federal government has been so bureaucratized that the cities and the states could do better on their own deciding how to use the money, and not have that federal interference. There was always great rhetoric about how the cities and states know their needs better than the federal government, and should not have to write applications and such. The Administration planned all along that there would be no qualifications other than a simple entitlement, based on certain criteria. There is no application to be filed to receive the money.

It comes as a check in the mail to the city. In a few cases cities and towns did not know what to do with it, so they just sent it back!

There is no monitoring of expenditures. The federal government is not going to come back and challenge the spending. The only thing in the law that is restrictive in nature is the usual flower thrown to civil rights. If there were a case where a city spent money only in all white areas and not black areas, a law suit alleging that this money was spent in contravention to the Civil Rights Act of 1964 might be sustained.

When General Revenue Sharing was proposed by the Nixon Administration, it was part of a larger package. First it was part of the philosophy of the New Federalism. The reason that it is called *General* Revenue Sharing is that along with it went a proposal for six *special* revenue sharing programs. In other words the Administration was not just going to take the approach of giving money out for the cities to use for any purposes, especially for the reduction in taxes. They wanted some monies available for the typical areas that the government had been assisting—transportation, community development, economic development, health, education, and welfare. There would be six *special* revenue sharing packages. All the grant-in-aid programs would be eliminated, and the cities would be given entitlements for these special revenue sharing plans. Tied to the special revenue sharing package was a proposal to restructure completely the Executive Branch of the Government. The cabinet level officers would have responsibility for the new special revenue sharing areas.

The whole program got out of kilter because it involved restructuring of the government. The Congress resisted. Since the amounts of money proposed by the Nixon Administration for each of these areas were significantly less than what cities and states were getting under the categorical programs, they could not even get the reorganization bills introduced. The only special revenue sharing bills which made it were those dealing with Manpower and Community Development. That is how Housing and Community Development got tied in to General Revenue Sharing.

What was the opposition? The main opponent was Wilbur Mills. His views represented many people and the fundamental problems they had with Revenue Sharing. First, even though Congressmen say the federal bureaucracy is too big, and they do not want any strings attached, actually when they get down to appropriating monies, they *do* want the federal government to be responsible for what happens to that money. It is political instinct. It always happens. After all, the voters are going to hold the Congressman responsible for the monies he appropriates, and he knows that. The Congressman may say, "I don't want the federal government telling anybody what to do." But if he is going to appropriate that money, he wants someone to be accountable for it. It does not seem right that the federal government would levy the tax and then give it back to somebody who did not raise that tax, Mills argued, and many agreed with him. But the mayors and governors turned him around.

Significant Congressional prerogative was given up in Revenue Sharing. The Congress always resists appropriating for more than one year. It was a big battle with Model Cities. HUD tried first to get a five year appropriation; Congress would not go for that—it had to appropriate each year. With Revenue Sharing, however, they did give up that prerogative—because after all, the states and the cities did require some idea of the continuity of the program to know what they could depend on. Congress created a trust fund with a five year life span for which the Secretary of the Treasury has been designated as trustee. No one has to go back to the Congress each year and ask for the money. Every city and state knows how much it is going to get. A specified proportion of income tax revenues is diverted each year into this trust fund, and then it is divided according to population and characteristics of the cities and states.

Another criticism comes from the people who represent the views of the needy. Part of the Nixon strategy with Revenue Sharing was to strengthen the surburban areas. It became an issue of the central city versus the suburbs. After all, most localities are not central cities. And most people do not live in the central city. You can make the philosophical argument that the people with the greatest needs ought to get the greatest amount. But, with revenue sharing those with the least need receive the greatest amount since the amount is based upon population. There were attempts by the more liberal Congressmen and Senators to weight the formula with poverty and overcrowded housing indicators. They were not successful.

What then, is the impact of General Revenue Sharing on urban problems? Perhaps it is best summed up in the following exerpt from a bulletin published in 1974 by the National Housing and Economic Development Law Project at Berkeley, California:

Funds from revenue sharing may significantly augment taxes collected in the jurisdiction since revenue for rural jurisdictions are based on both lower rates of taxation and a smaller amount of taxable property or income than is available in urban jurisdictions. However, with the possible exception of the local housing authorities which stand on the brink of financial chaos, the impact of general revenue sharing on urban areas will simply not be that great. In this regard, it is important to understand that the central characteristic of this legislation is that it is "free" money with no strings attached. It is money which can be used by the local governmental unit to pay policemen, purchase fire trucks, build schools or to redecorate the mayor's office. Perhaps a more critical formulation of the problem for those interested in social and community development programs in urban areas would be: How would these programs expect to fare from new funds available to the states or cities as a result of a rise in property or sales taxes which augmented the city's or state's available revenue by five percent to ten percent?

Without significant reforms in the nation's social service delivery and welfare system, the benefits of revenue sharing may in some cases be short lived. Aside from the fact that the need of local governments for additional revenue far outstrips the projected five year outlays authorized by the general revenue sharing legislation (i.e., only a minor part of a deficit is being closed with these funds), even this contribution could be cut back in the mistaken belief that revenue sharing is alleviating the local government financial crisis.

The most obvious manifestation of this threat can be found on the face of the legislation. In Title III of the legislation, Congress placed severe limitations on federal contributions to local social service and welfare programs. While matching funds for "workfare" programs will continue to be available to states, Congress zeroed in on one of its favorite targets, the AFDC program. The compromise between the two Houses as to the limitation on matching funds for social service programs took the following forms according to the conference committee report:

> Under the substitute, Federal matching for social services under programs of aid to the aged, blind, and disabled, and aid to families with dependent children would be subject to a State-by-State dollar limitation, effective beginning with fiscal year 1973. Each state would be limited to its share of $2,500,000,000 based on its proportion of population in the United States.

The immediate consequences of this limitation will be felt far beyond just those social service programs which will have matching fund constraints imposed. For example, in many instances the ceiling on federal contribution means that states and localities which supply the local share will have to reach into the funds they receive from revenue sharing to support those programs subject to the federal share limitation if the current budget levels for individual recipients are to be maintained at present levels. While this phenomenon for the time being is limited to the large industrial states where benefit levels are high, it does point up the fact that revenue sharing can be used as a double-edge sword with respect to other social programs. Hopefully, however, the revenue sharing funds, limited though they may be, will only be used for meeting the needs of local government and not as convenient rationales for placing the burden of funding costly and "unpopular" social programs on the local governmental units which are in no position to afford even more "acceptable" ones.

While the overall probability of obtaining revenue sharing funds for social and community development programs (with the possible exception of public housing) is low, it does not mean that revenue sharing should be ignored either on the local or national level. In some instances governors, mayors, and county officials have not specified plans for using the incremental funds. It is possible that they may welcome innovative or flexible suggestions for programmatic uses of the funds, especially during the next year or so, since no long-range plans have been made (and there is some fear of not being able to use the funds wisely). Yet, even where there are no hard and fast plans for using the revenue sharing funds, any demands by low-income community groups will have to be presented as being politically more worthwhile than the simple and appealing expedient of cutting property taxes. (This, of course, will require creative planning and political pressure locally.)[1]

In the long run, the issue to which Wilbur Mills and others point was important—accountability. The accountability issue will influence Congress when it considers the extension of revenue sharing. If there are examples such as are heard when foreign aid is discussed—those wild things that are financed, there might be a backlash. Therefore, it is imperative for the local governments to try to balance interests and serve not just those who are in control of the city but those who have the most need.

It is instructive to observe the way the Administration got revenue sharing passed. In 1969 the Administration began acting like revenue sharing was already a reality. As much as possible they changed the structure of the federal system by cutting the grant-in-aid programs. The best example of this is the housing moratorium. They said, "We want community development passed under the special revenue sharing package." But Wilbur Mills and other people in Congress were resisting it. So the Administration said, "You either have community development or nothing because we are going to cut out all of these programs whether you, Congress, agree or not." And so they threatened to stop these programs. It was "take it or leave it." The same thing was happening with general revenue sharing. The cities were being cut back and in the end, the mayors were in the position of beggars saying, "We have to take this or nothing."

Can general revenue sharing help cities provide housing? Cities are receiving this revenue sharing money—why can't they use that for housing, since the other categorical programs have been cut out? The same question is asked at the state level. The answer is that the commitment from the federal government to general revenue sharing is five years. Community Development funds were also authorized for five years. If the money is used as subsidy what it going to happen at the end of five years? It is not enough money to finance housing. The point is that general revenue sharing may not be long term money, which housing financing requires. Revenue sharing could be used to augment a city's efforts—such as paying the deficits incurred by local housing authorities, but its main contribution to housing is to help cities pay for the sewers, waterlines, streets, and other facilities which are the necessary bases on which housing can be built.

VIII. STATE HOUSING PROGRAMS: NEW TOOLS TO PRODUCE HOUSING

Just a few years ago, the idea of the states playing a significant role in the housing field was foreign.

The Constitution gives the states all powers not reserved to the federal government. But state government involvement in urban problems has been minimal. The states, of course, from the late 18th and through the 19th Century, were formed and had their character stamped on them by rural society. The Supreme Court decision in 1962, *Baker v. Carr*, required the states to reapportion their legislatures, based on the principle of one man——one vote. In a subsequent reapportionment case in 1964, Chief Justice Earl Warren wrote, "Legislators represent people, not trees or acres. Legislators are elected by voters, not farms or cities or economic interests."[1]

The states' legislatures were notoriously rurally dominated. But from the New Deal days to the present a steady motion of force at the federal level flowed from the legislation passed in Congress concerning human welfare. On the other hand, the cities were facing the problems to which the federal government was responding. The states were sitting out this tremendous social upheaval of centralization of power in Washington and deepening problems faced by the cities. It became a cliche in the 50's and 60's to say that the cities were in financial stress. Why was that? The crisis of the cities was that they faced the portentous problems of urban growth while shackled by their creators, the states. They have no power outside what the states delegate to them.

The most blatant case of how the city is hobbled, hindered, and given obstacles is the city of Detroit which is the fifth largest city and probably has problems as serious as any in the country. It has a militant racial situation which all came to fireworks in 1967 and yet the city of Detroit has no power to raise its taxes without the state government giving its blessing. That is just the most blatant example, but it is the character of a situation that is repeated throughout the country. The cities are creatures of the states, but the states have often hindered them from doing their job, like meeting their problems of housing, welfare, education, and transportation. Thus, the states have been a positive deterrent to amelioration of urban social problems.

With this record in mind, it is anomalous that the role of the states in housing is now significant. Why would they become involved? First, problems in the cities caused the industrialized states to respond and so a pattern began to be set in the 1960's with respect to housing and urban development. Naturally the first state to do something was New York. In 1960 New York established a state housing finance agency. The agency was a creature of the state legislature, empowered to sell revenue bonds, to finance the construction of housing for moderate income people. Urban Renewal was a stimulus to the states in awakening them to some responsibilities; for instance, the necessity to raise capital was beyond the means of many localities, and in states such as New York, Connecticut, New Jersey, Massachusetts, places which had an interest in Urban Renewal and wanted to have the cities participate, those states passed laws granting some funds to pay the local share of Urban Renewal. That was in the 50's. It laid the groundwork for this first move by a state, New York, to get more directly involved in housing. Now, of course, New York itself had some historical precedent. In 1955 the state had established the Mitchell-Lama Program, under which the state would borrow money and make loans to developers at a lower than market rate interest to build housing for middle-income people.

After New York stated in 1960 twelve other states passed such laws and set up housing finance agencies in the next ten years. In the 60's thirteen states had these agencies—not a large number—and all of those were basically the eastern and northern industrial states. They were responding to the needs of their cities; the request of their cities to build housing for low and moderate income families. If one were a Congressman from the Bronx or from Brooklyn, one would have been concerned when housing bills were passed in the Congress because your district could have used every dime appropriated. Hugh Carey, who is now the Governor, and Williams Fitts Ryan made speeches about how their districts' problem of housing were so great that they could use the entire appropriation under the Public Housing Act. This, of course, was true. The people from Idaho, Iowa, and Wyoming would put in the Acts that no state could receive more than 15 percent of the total appropriation. This was a slap in the face to New Yorkers. From their perspective, the federal programs were totally inadequate. So there was pressure on states to augment these programs. Mississippi, Alabama, and

Colorado, by and large, do not want the federal housing programs. But with states like New York, there is more pressure than can be met by the federal government. There is pressure at the state level and the state responded. The movement for state housing finance agencies really began to catch on in the early 1970's.

Why did it catch on? First, when Congress enacted the Housing Act of 1968, a tremendous mechanism, the 236 program, was set up which could amplify and augment the efforts of those states with housing agencies. The states had the capacity, by selling revenue bonds, to raise the long term capital, and the federal government on the other hand was passing out money by the millions to subsidize moderate income housing.

Representative Ryan of New York in 1965 started trying to get the subsidies under the Rent Supplement Program to apply to state financed housing, not just federally insured housing. The Rent Supplement was tied to a Section 221 (d) (3) Federally Insured Market Rate Mortgage. Why not let that subsidy apply to state financed housing as well, he asked. But Congress would not buy that until 1968. It took three years of Ryan's hammering to finally get a specific sentence into the Housing Act of 1968 saying that the subsidy could apply to state-financed housing.

The 1968 Act immediately gave the New York Housing Finance Agency and all of the others a piggy back tool, by which they could make a loan to a developer with interest rates below the market. It could be about 4 or 5 percent in 1969 and 1970. This low interest rate already was a subsidy. Then they also took a subsidy from 236, to bring the interest rate down to 1 percent. FHA was subsidizing a 4 or 5 percent mortgage, so the dollars went further. Through March 1, 1973, these housing finance agencies accounted for 46,632 units of 236 housing, a hefty load for basically twelve or thirteen agencies to put out. Other states saw that states with finance agencies had a double subsidy going. In 1970, 1971, and 1972, the dramatic, revolutionary increase in housing production was witnessed by state planners and state legislators. Since 1970, twenty-five other states have enacted laws setting up housing finance agencies and today there are thirty-eight in existence. Most of the other states which do not have state housing finance agencies are not going to do any housing anyway, like Idaho and Montana. All the big states and many of the small states like Georgia and Mississippi have these agencies.

So much for the historical perspective. There is another situation, a less happy situation. Which ironically argues strongly for the creation of these agencies. If state housing agencies were important during the era of great production under 236, they are indispensable today when HUD comes out with a new leasing program under Section 8, which has no means to subsidize the financing and the construction of housing. It only deals with the subsidy of the tenant once he is in the unit. What is going to happen with respect to the financing? This is where the state powers and state agencies would not be so important if it were not for the fact that the other two means of financing housing to lease to the housing authority have little viability. Conventional financing is almost impossible due to scarcity of money. FHA financing, if it were available, is too expensive. The FHA rate is 8½ percent plus ½ percent for the mortgage insurance. However, in early 1976, the Ford Aministration announced a "Tandem Plan" for multifamily construction. This allows for a 7½ percent mortgage and a limit of 2½ discount points. HUD spokesmen stated that the Tandem approach was designed to make more feasible FHA financing of Section 8 projects.

The third alternative is financing by a state housing finance agency.

It is feasible because revenue bonds can be sold for about 8 percent. Unfortunately, the ripples of UDC's failure have washed over the entire bond market, and state housing agency issues have experienced great difficulties in terms of ratings and marketability.

As a remedy for this difficulty, State agencies have pressed the Federal Government to assist by coinsuring the bonds, so as to overcome the rather damaged "moral obligation" pledge of States, and give bond purchases an added security device.

As an additional incentive to the states, in the 1974 Act the Congress allowed the states to sell *taxable* revenue bonds, rather than tax-exempt revenue bonds. The buyer of the bonds has to pay taxes, but the federal government will in turn subsidize to the agency 3 points on whatever it takes to sell those taxable revenue bonds.

The subsidy does not apply to the buyer of the bonds. The state agency goes out on the market and sells taxable bonds, paying an interest rate of 10 percent and the buyer pays taxes according to his income level on that 10 percent. Back home, the agency which is having to pay out the 10 percent is getting a check from the U. S. Government amounting to 3 percent of that, which makes it possible then for them to loan the money to developers at probably 2 percent under the 10 percent. They loan it at 8 percent. HUD has steadily opposed this section of the 1974 Housing Act, and has instead entered into discussions about the coinsurance program mentioned above. So, even if HUD again shows its disdain for the law, at least it recognizes that State financing is the most viable mechanism for Section 8.

An additional incentive in the Housing and Community Development Act allows the state housing finance agencies not only to be the financer for leased housing under the new Section 8 but to be the actual subsidizer. The state itself will get the money and distribute it. It will choose the site and the developer, loan him money, and subsidize his tenants once he is in operation. Now all of this did not happen by accident. The man who wrote that part of the bill was formerly the head of the Illinois Housing Development Authority, Daniel Kearney. He later served as head of the Government National Mortgage Association. He has advocated a stronger role for the states in housing finance.

The main function of a state housing finance agency is to make loans. The money it loans is raised by selling tax exempt revenue bonds. Normally the legislation which establishes one of these agencies limits the bonding authority of the agency to a certain dollar amount. These bonds are not backed by the federal government. They are not even backed by the full faith and credit of the state government. It is not like selling a bond to finance a river. If the water authority runs into any kind of a problem and cannot sell its water to industrial users along the channels that it serves, the state government pays off the bond holders. A housing agency bond is not like that kind of bond. The bonds are backed by: 1) the project, such that if the project fails, the bond holder is not paid. 2) A moral obligation clause in the legislation states that the governor, with the advice of the housing finance board, will report to the legislature any deficits in the reserve funds of the authority. It is assumed that the legislature has the moral obligation to make up those deficits by appropriations. But there is nothing in the statutes which commands, or demands, that they do that.

The states have built management into their projects much better than the federal government ever did. Looking back it is almost inscrutable how Congress and HUD could get into a program like 236 which they did in 1969 and 1970, 1971, and have no concept of what it takes to manage them. The states did not do that; their management programs have been very strong, especially in Michigan. Michigan has a form of management which is being copied all over the country. They have put out literature on housing management. In other words, the state-financed housing projects are

50 percent better than the federally subsidized because of good management. The political criticism has been on other grounds—location of the projects. Westchester County did not want any state-financed housing. The same was true of Michigan; Grosse Pointe did not want any either. So, there has been resistance because the states have taken an active role. They have produced 250,000 units of housing in the last five years and that is an active role, and so, activists create re-activists. There has been criticism but it has not been on the basis of bad management.

Another Personal Note

In Texas a housing finance agency bill was first introduced in 1971. It was introduced under the aegis of a private group that the Governor appointed, called the Texas Urban Development Commission. On that committee was Mr. H. B. Zachry, who is a very large contractor; he usually builds highways and bridges. He is the largest contractor in Texas except for Brown and Root—he is from San Antonio. He is a very headstrong man of about seventy and he got it into his mind that the housing problems of Texas could be solved if he could, like he did with the Palacio Del Rio Hotel in San Antonio, build little modules out of concrete and have every poor person in Texas living in a concrete house. He wanted a bill written to effectuate this complete eradication of the slums of Texas. And he got support from no less a man than Tom Sealy, a former big gun in politics in Texas, and formerly associated with John Connally's law firm. So Tom Sealy and John Connally drafted him a bill. After he told them what he wanted to do, they sat down and looked around and they saw that what he wanted was an urban development corporation in Texas with powers of eminent domain. He even wanted to have the powers of eminent domain without judicial review of the condemnation proceedings, which in legal circles is unthinkable. Not to have judicial review of a condemnation action by a public body is not possible, but he thought that landlords were ripping off people. He thought they should have a right to protest what was being done by their landlords. The Zachry bill would never pass, but he was a very powerful man. He was paying out of his own pocket very expensive lawyers to do the bill, and here was the bill being written, and I got involved in trying to answer some of the questions raised during the drafting. It leaked out to the press that this kind of bill was being written. Mr. Zachry sat down with the Governor, Lieutenant Governor, and Speaker, and told them he wanted this bill passed and they said, "Yes Sir."

They got Barbara Jordan in the Senate to put her name on it. All of a sudden some legislators from San Antonio who did not like Zachry got some word about this bill being passed. The Head of the AFL/CIO was on the Urban Development Commission and it occurred to him that it was going to be a slave labor program because Zachry is a nonunion contractor.

Meanwhile, I and others were working on a housing finance agency bill. It had no opposition and was sailing right through in the House Committee after being passed in the Senate, and it came up for a vote in the House. There was actually a procedural question to put it on the calendar. This was about two days before the end of the 1971 Session of the Legislature, and the housing finance agency bill was being voted on and all the lights were green—YES, there were no "NO's." They had all turned green and now they were all turning red. Hawkins Menefee and I ran down to the floor to find out why all of a sudden the lights were turning red. Some legislators were saying "This is the Zachry Bill, this is the Zachry Bill!" The San Antonio legislators had been spreading that rumor all around over the floor of the House. Most of the legislators did not know what they were voting on, and those who were against the bill had been spreading that rumor, so when they said, "This is the Zachry bill," they all changed their vote and voted NO. They voted down the housing finance agency bill because they thought it was the Zachry Bill. We did get it back on the calendar two days later, but time ran out before it was voted on.

The State Housing Finance Agency bill was again considered in the 1973 Session of the Texas Legislature, but failed to gain approval. And in 1975, because of the dramatic changes in attitude caused by the federal moratorium, prospects looked bright for enactment of the bill—until the catastrophic failure of the New York Urban Development Corporation cast a pall over the future of "moral obligation" bonds. UDC was unable to pay holders of bonds for several hundreds of millions of dollars. UDC, unlike state housing finance agencies, is a developer, not merely a lender, and it became clear that it could not finish the projects it had under construction without raising many more millions of dollars. Confidence with Wall Street was shattered, and unfortunately the pessimism seems to have spilled over to all types of "moral obligation" issues, even though a state housing finance agency issues bonds on a specific project, not for the operating of a total development program as the UDC did. So, for now, the prospects for state programs to assist housing are quite bleak.

I believe that the wisest words about the UDC's fall are those of Joseph Fried, who writes on housing for *The New York Times*. In an article in *The Nation*, August 16, 1975 he said,

Rebuilding the slums is a long-term and financially risky endeavor at best, one in which reverses will be suffered, mistakes made and money lost—just as mistakes are made and money is wasted in mindlessly building and rebuilding the kind of weapons structure deemed vital by the Pentagon and its boosters in Congress.

Fried goes on to say that only after a full report is published will one know whether Edward Logue and his staff took undue risks in guiding UDC's program, but Fried believes, as I do, that no man or organization, even one as formidable as the UDC, can be expected to rely completely on the private investment market, which is "skittish and volatile, buffeted as much by psychological forces and currents as by economic conditions." Rather, Fried argues, "the job (of wiping out slums) must be done by American society generally, and that means sufficient public funds for subsidized housing and redevelopment programs to begin with, *as well as a willingness by government to take the ultimate risk when it does seek to draw private capital into the effort.*" (Emphasis Added)

As the housing crisis deepens and production of housing for lower-income families remains stagnant, perhaps public pressures for a revived housing industry will bring the state agencies back to their important place in housing finance.

IX. COMMUNITY DEVELOPMENT:
NIXON'S IRONIC VICTORY

The enactment of the Housing and Community Development Act has opened exciting prospects for the cities. It is an $8.4 billion program, and every city in America must figure out what to do with its entitlement.

Title I of the Housing and Community Development Act created a new program called Community Development which became effective January 1, 1975. That effective date itself was another item of debate in Congress. HUD had carried the cities along for such a long period of time in limbo as a way to have leverage on the Congress. In 1972 they told cities to start acting like they had community development. But Community Development did not pass the Congress; it did pass the Senate, but it did not pass the House in 1972, so HUD had to get an extension of monies to continue Urban Renewal and Model Cities, and the other physical development programs. It was a paltry amount, and therefore crippled Urban Renewal and Model Cities.

As an example, in Houston the second Action Year of Model Cities was to run through December of 1972, and it was fully expected by HUD that on January 1, 1973, Revenue Sharing and Community Development would be in place and that Model Cities would therefore be terminated. But since the law was not enacted, and since it was pretty late in the 1972 Session when it became clear that it was not going to pass the House, HUD had to get some more money, so they extended the Model Cities program in Houston. This was happening all over the country. One month, two months, three months, four months, five months, finally the Houston Model Cities program was extended on a month-to-month basis through June of 1973. By that time it was obvious that there was not going to be a Community Development bill. HUD went ahead and got another appropriation for another year of Model Cities and Urban Renewal. So we had a Third Action Year beginning July 1, 1973. In 1974, after all this uncertainty, there were those who were pushing to enact Community Development as soon as possible so it could get underway quickly. The Senate wanted it to start in June of 1974 and passed its bill in March 1974. But the House did not get around to passing the bill until June because of the impeachment hearings. The conference lasted until the end of July and the bill did not get back to the floor of both Houses until the middle of August. By that time the June date was out of whack so they pushed it up to January 1975. The "effective date" is a relatively small point, but the small point unravels into the big issue of what kind of bill would pass.

Community Development replaces eight former categorical programs: water and sewer grants, urban renewal, urban beautification, public facility loans, model cities, historic preservation, neighborhood facilities grants, and concentrated code enforcement. It is important to note these programs because it is fully expected and intended that these programs be continued substantially as they are under the new rubric of Community Development. Cities are in the middle of these programs. Hundreds of Urban Renewal projects are in the middle of their lengthy process of acquisition, demolition, and development. Community Development funds will be used to finish these projects.

For instance, in Port Arthur, Texas 140 parcels of land remain from the Urban Renewal program. They are now having to find some way of disposing of these parcels. That is just a small example of what is happening all over the country: the cities have been held for over two years in limbo not knowing what to do with the land and plans of Urban Renewal projects. Now there is some hope that they can get on with the job. The cities will build on the past and will try to find ways to complete the projects which they had begun and on which so much energy has been spent. In some cases where Urban Renewal plans and projects were planned ten years ago, all the assumptions are ten years old. Hundreds of Urban Renewal projects across the country were stopped, because they were in mid-process, having to re-plan, re-tool because of the increased costs of financing and construction and not being able to because of the moratorium which in the case of Urban Renewal has been in effect since June of 1973.

The single significant point about Community Development is that categorical programs which required a separate application process are now replaced by a system of block grants in which the city itself determines what it wants to do with the funds rather than having to apply for a program which has a certain amount of money to do specific tasks. The old system required a choice by the federal government to award the application. Under Community Development, the city is entitled to its share.

HUD was not successful in its proposal to have no review process of the city's plans for using Community Development funds.

However, the House members were not successful either in getting a new type of review process based on the metropolitan planning concept. The Senate version of the review process was in the Act. The city does have to submit a Community Development plan. Although they have an entitlement, they must say how they are going to use it and HUD has to review it. HUD can look at the plans strictly or liberally. The HUD officials are going to take the position which they have taken in the beginning when the bill was proposed—to have the least amount of influence. They really do not want to get involved. This is the atmosphere in HUD now. Not to look at this like an Urban Renewal application, but simply to be a rubber stamp of what the city says it wants to do. If the city says it wants to do certain things and it says it in the correct English language, then HUD will put its stamp on it and let the cities go their way.

The "hold harmless" concept is the second important point. The cities are going to have some safeguard as to the amount of money they were getting under the old programs. Most large cities have been participating in these programs to such a degree that if their total is added, the amount would be greater than the amount under Community Development, because the formula is weighted in favor of where the Republicans are. The "hold harmless" provision is to protect the principal cities so that they will receive as much as they did under the old programs.

Who can get into this program? That is very important and also involved a good bit of debate. The House, for example, based on the Panel studies done by the House Sub-Committee on Housing in 1970-71, really wanted to strengthen the metropolitan planning process and wanted most of the grants to go to the metropolitan agencies. That was not acceptable to the Senate or to HUD. The result was that states, cities, counties, and other units of general local governments, in addition to public agencies designated by HUD, such as new communities, Indian Tribes, Alaskan Indians, Eskimos, all were included as eligible recipients.

Since Community Development is a special Revenue Sharing program, it has some broad outlines as to what is to be accomplished. The Act does spell out certain activities which are expected to be funded. It is not just *carte blanche* like general revenue sharing.

The Act lists specific activities:

1. Acquisition of real property, that is, property which is blighted, deteriorated, deteriorating, or inappropriately

developed. What a terrific planner's phrase, "inappropriately developed."

2. Acquisition of property appropriate for rehabilitation and conservation activities. This tracks in the first case Urban Renewal and in the second case Concentrated Code Enforcement, which gives the language for cities to continue that type of activity.

3. Acquisition of property which is appropriate for preservation or restoration of historical sites, urban beautification, conservation of open spaces, natural resources or scenic areas, recreation, or the guidance of urban development. This tracks the urban beautification and historic preservation programs.

4. Acquisition of property which is to be used for the provision of eligible public works facilities and improvement. This tracks the water and sewer grants and public facility loans program.

5. Acquisition of property which is to be used for other public purposes. Quite a catch all!

The other general activity allowed under the Act is the acquisition, construction, or installation of public works including neighborhood and senior citizens' facilities, historic properties, street lights, water and sewer, foundations for air rights sites, malls and walk ways, and recreational facilities. Flood and drainage facilities are eligible only where a system under other federal programs is unavailable. Parking, solid waste disposal facilities, and fire protection, are eligible only in cases where they are serving related community development areas. This comes out of a concept in the Urban Renewal program—the Act tries to limit what the city does with Urban Renewal or in this case Community Development money when really the city should be using its own money.

Other eligible activities are code enforcement, involving clearance, demolition, removal, and rehabilitation improvements. Interim assistance and financing the rehabilitation of privately owned properties is allowed. Also, special projects to remove material and architectural barriers restricting mobility and accessibility of elderly and handicapped persons, payments to housing owners for loss of rental income while temporarily holding units in use for relocation, disposition of acquired real property, and provision of public services necessary to support such activities. Under the Urban Renewal program it was soon discovered that if the city goes into a neighborhood and buys up houses, relocates people, tears down houses, builds new houses, then a whole series of problems and needs immediately arise. For instance, there is a period in which the city owns houses—there are people to relocate, there are people who cannot find a house for some time. They cannot move into just any house, but one they choose after being presented with some alternatives. So, the cities get involved in repairs just like a landlord, even such things as providing day care for the people who live in the city's properties, or transportation for elderly persons. The whole gamut of responsibilities of being the owner of property fall to the city. The new Act tries to help them meet their obligations.

Another eligible activity is payment of the non-federal share in connection with other federal programs undertaken as a part of the development program. Community Development is similar to Model Cities also in that there is no matching requirement by the city. The Community Development grant is a 100 percent grant. This was a significant point in the legislative history. The Senators wanted the cities to put up a match to get Community Development, but the House did not.

Payments for relocation are allowed, including activities necessary to develop a comprehensive plan and a policy plan and management capacity to determine more effectively objectives and set goals. This is an improvement over the past because under Urban Renewal or Model Cities, the planning process itself was paid for out of preliminary funds which had to be applied for. In Community Development the city determines how many planners and how much money it wants to spend out of the general pot.

Lastly, payment of reasonable administrative costs and carrying charges related to the planning and distribution of activities. Again, an Urban Renewal agency each year would have to appeal and apply to HUD to support its administrative budget. This is avoided now. The Act also spells out the things which cannot be supported by Community Development funds:

1. Public facilities not a part of a Community Development plan.
2. Operating and maintenance expenses, except in connection with authorized public services. In other words a city cannot use this money to pay for the fire department, the sanitary sewer program, or any other program ordinarily funded by the city's tax revenues.
3. General government expenses.
4. Political activities.
5. New housing construction.
6. Income supplement payments.

What does the city have to do to get the funds? They have to submit a *Community Development plan summary for three years.* Why is it for three years? Because that is how long the authorization lasts. That is how long there is going to be a program insofar as the authorized funds are there. This Community Development summary is supposed to identify the Community Development needs, demonstrate a comprehensive strategy for meeting the needs, and specify short and long term objectives. The plan must demonstrate how the community will attack the problems of slums, blight, deterioration, and demonstrate how the community will use the plan to encompass needs, strategies and objectives necessary to provide improved community development facilities.

In all these plans the city must take into account special needs of low-income persons—limit the Community Development funds to those most in need. Congress often does this. For instance, the rent supplement program was first proposed by President Johnson in 1965 as a moderate income program, not for low income, and was to be used to disperse moderate income people into the suburbs. The dispersal aspect was objectionable, of course, to many. But more objectionable was that it was for moderate income families. It was immediately turned around into a low income program. It is that kind of mentality which operates in Congress when a housing act comes up. These specific sentences put in for emphasis on the low and moderate income are in the Community Development Act. The HUD officials did not want any strings. They wanted it to be like general revenue sharing, to be a tool by which the suburban community of basically middle class citizens which is caught by inadequate sewer and water facilities and spiralling property taxes would have a way to keep those taxes from going up, and still provide the services and facilities needed. It would not be limited to low income people.

In addition to the Community Development summary, which is a three-year outline, the city must submit a *Community Development Program* which is a one-year action plan. They must submit a program which includes activities to meet the community development needs and objectives along with the estimated costs and general location of such activity. The latter must be shown on maps outlining census tracts or standard numeration districts which include prevailing population characteristics. The program outline must also indicate other sources of funding which will be used toward the completion of the plan and take environmental factors into account. In other words, it has to be fairly detailed, what the acitivities are going to be, how much it is going to cost, where it is going to be done.

Third, the city must submit a *housing assistance plan*. The housing assistance plan must accurately survey the conditions of the community's housing stock and housing needs of lower income persons.

The city must specify a realistic annual goal for the number of housing units for persons to be assisted, including new, existing and rehabilitated units and the size and types of projects and assistance best suited for the provision of housing for lower-income families.

The housing assistance plan must indicate the general location of proposed lower income housing with a view to furthering the vitalization of blighted areas, promoting greater housing choice, avoiding undue concentration of low income persons, and assuring availability of adequate public facilities and services for such housing.

The housing program is the fatal flaw of this Act. The process of planning for Community Development provides a wide choice as to what to do and how to do it and where to do it. But in respect to housing what is there to attack the problem? One program—Section 8 Leasing for poor people.

The first thing the cities are going to learn is that there are many, many people who live in areas that will be designated as community development areas who are not poor under the terms of the Act. That is to say, they are not 80 percent below median income. But, what does it matter that you are not 80 percent below median income level, and yet have no possible way on earth to buy or rent a house, which is the case with three-fourths of the American families right now? Of course, all of them are not so poor as to say they are at 80 percent of the median. So, the housing assistance program is only going to attack a part, and really a small part, because, after all, the lower-middle class are more numerous than the poor. The only weapon in the arsenal will support only the poorest. In short, the cities need the full panoply of federal housing programs, but they are hobbled by the effects of the moratorium.

The Congress has stated its reaction to the moratorium in several different ways and on several different occasions: 1) they have stated it in this Act. There is a one-year additional authorization for Section 236 and 235. The authorization is less than what the Senators wanted, but it is certainly more than what HUD or the House wanted. In other words, they have repudiated the moratorium by saying we hereby authorize 236 and 235 for one year. 2) They also passed a very important Act last session of Congress which was the overall response to the whole question of impoundment, the Budget and Impoundment Control Act, which states that the President is not empowered to impound funds without first notifying Congress and setting up a whole system of procedures to follow. They included some responsibility about budgeting by the Congress. But that was a general response to impoundment—they rejected impoundment as a procedure and specifically they rejected the housing moratorium. 3) In addition, many of the Senators individually joined in a suit in the federal courts to challenge the moratorium on housing. The U. S. Appeals Court of the District of Columbia in August 1974, a few days prior to the passage of the Act, ruled against them. In this case, which was decided around the first of August, the Court vindicated Secretary Lynn who said, "I do not have to reinstate the programs." Then the Act passed and the Congress directed him to reinstate, and Lynn's answer was that the courts had upheld him and he did not have to obey the Congress. The day after the Act HUD immediately sent all the field offices a memo which stated that they were not to process any 236 and 235 applications.

HUD, in that memo, did say to the offices that if under the housing assistance plan which is submitted by the city, it is determined that only 236 is serviceable, then they can make application for a certain number of units of 236.

The opinion of the U. S. District Court of Appeals was a travesty. It was truly shocking because the judges did not wait until the Congress had acted and expressed its will about the housing programs. The whole brunt of the argument was that HUD did not have to implement these programs because the intent of Congress was not being followed. HUD was not about to say that Congress made a big mistake, that Congress did not know what it was doing. So they said these programs did not accomplish what the Congress intended. If the Court had waited a few days they would have seen that the Congress reiterated its confidence in the programs. As far as supporting their own arguments in favor of HUD, the judges quoted from the HUD publication *Housing in the Seventies*, which HUD had put out in September 1973 to justify the moratorium. The study is no more than a propaganda piece for the moratorium. Most readers immediately labeled it as self-serving. But it served as the judges' authoritative source. Of course they do not deal with housing every day or even once a year for that matter. And they look at something that is put out by the Government, by HUD, and they have confidence in it. The study made the projection that 40 percent of all the 236's are going to be in foreclosure in ten years. There were no grounds for that argument—how do they justify it? That is the kind of thing that the judges quoted, and of course, after they made their decision, many people wrote letters trying to tell them that the document was so in error, but by that time it was too late. So it remains that the Community Development program may be fatally flawed by an unworkable housing program, and the cities stand vulnerable to the same trap they fell into with Urban Renewal —they had a popular and effective redevelopment tool, but the lack of housing continually revealed the problems of relocation and segregation of minorities and the poor.

To carry out their Community Development Program the cities must:

1. Comply with civil rights laws.
2. Provide citizens with "adequate" information concerning the amount of funds available for Community Development and housing activity, the range of activities, and other important requirements of the program. The city must hold public hearings to obtain the views of the citizens on Community Development and housing. They must provide citizens with adequate opportunity to participate in the development of the application. As with general revenue sharing, there is no structure required and very little criteria for what is adequate participation. It is not like Model Cities, which was very stringent in this respect. Model Cities was similar to the OEO requirement of "maximum feasible participation." The Community Development Act does not contain such lofty idealism.
3. The cities have to comply with all federal relocation policies and statutes. The Uniform Relocation Act of 1969 which applies to this program is very demanding.
4. Another important requirement: compliance with the provisions of the National Environmental Policy Act—which means an environmental impact statement has to be supplied by the city.
5. The Plan and the implementation must give maximum priority to benefit low or moderate income families. In other words, there is going to be a cause of action by representatives of the poor if it can be shown that cities avoided that requirement.

The Housing and Community Development Act of 1974 was passed in its final form only a few days after the historic resignation of Richard Nixon. As Kenneth R. Harney stated in the *Housing and Development Reporter*, the timing of the two events was ironic because the Housing and Community Development Act is the "most noteworthy domestic triumph of the Nixon philosophy during the past four years." The Act accomplished two objectives the White House most wanted in the housing field: First, the Act replaces old categorical programs, which was what Nixon intended with the Special Revenue Sharing concept, and second, the Act, as Harney says, "accepts almost wholesale the conclusions reached by the Administration during the 1973 housing moratorium that leasing should be the country's sole large scale solution."

It remains to be seen whether Nixon's ironic victory will also be a victory for the cities of America—after three years of forced inaction, they deserve some better days in their relentless struggle against decay and disorder.

X. HOUSING THE AMERICAN PEOPLE

The late months of 1974 and early 1975 saw the results of a totally ravaged housing market—housing starts at their lowest since the Depression, interest rates at their highest in history, millions of American families forced to put aside any dreams to improve their housing condition. It is true that the housing picture has always brightened after "down" periods in the cycle—for example, 1966 and 1969. But the housing debacle of 1974-75 was too severe, too deep and far ranging to allow hope for a healthy recovery, without the insertion of new blood into the housing process.

For 1974-75 saw the collapse of positive federal involvement in housing production. John Ehrlichman's words in 1973 that "no one will be hurt" by the moratorium on subsidized housing now appear wantonly cruel. No less than two million lower-income families have been denied a decent home because of the "no production" policy of HUD. Millions of middle class Americans, many of them moving to new towns and cities, have been frustrated in their attempt to buy or rent a home in accord with their needs.

Unemployment in the construction trades climbed to 30 percent in some areas and averaged 20 percent across the country. Thousands of construction workers have had to find other sources of labor and will never return to construction.

The demise of housing production comes at precisely the time when the housing needs of the American people are becoming more dramatic.

Housing Needs in America

A recent study by the M.I.T.-Harvard Joint Center for Urban Studies points to the 13.1 million American families, or 21 percent of the Nation's 61.4 million households, which are "housing deprived," because of either living in poor housing, being overcrowded, or paying more than one-fourth of their income for housing.

The study also predicts that in this decade 23 million new dwelling units will be constructed; however, these units will only fill the needs of those "who can pay their own way," and will not help the "housing deprived." These, say the study director, Bernard J. Frieden, "must be considered a special challenge."

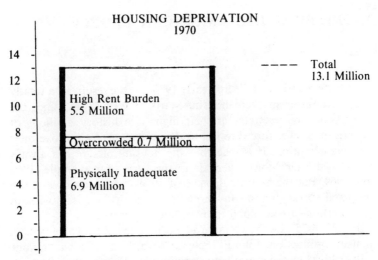

HOUSING DEPRIVATION
1970

- - - - Total
13.1 Million

High Rent Burden
5.5 Million

Overcrowded 0.7 Million

Physically Inadequate
6.9 Million

ROUGHLY 21 PERCENT of all households in the US are shown to experience some form of housing deprivation. Categories are estimated in non-overlapping terms—i.e., a household experiencing more than one problem is counted only once. Households of $10,000 and above were not included in the national estimate of deprivation.

The Nixon and Ford Administrations have not responded to the "special challenge," although it is true that many of these "housing deprived" families could benefit from some sort of housing allowance—at least 5.5 million of them who now live in decent homes, but have a high rent burden. But, over 7 million need *better quality* housing, and only a few of them will benefit from the trickle-down of better housing from those who move on to new homes.

The Revolution in the Housing Market

The deepening housing needs of Americans converge with the unprecedented changes in the structure of the housing market. An article in the November 1974 *Forbes* caught the essence of this revolution—"The Great American House Party is Over." The article illustrates why the party is over:

> Add up the higher cost of money and the higher cost of houses and you discover that the man lucky enough to have bought a typical house in 1967 would be paying around $140 a month on the mortgage; in 1974 the same house with a mortgage at 11% would require monthly payments of about $285. Looked at this way, the cost of buying a house has doubled in just seven years. Add rising taxes, fuel, utility and repair bills and it is clear that for most, the American dream house has been priced

out of the family market . . . out of 72 million households today, only 19 million, or 26%, have the necessary income of $15,000 or more required to buy the median new house at around $36,000.

The anomaly is that just when more and more American families become financial cripples in the race for housing, the finish line is pushed farther down the track.

A Faulty Answer to the Need

HUD, under Nixon and Ford, has stressed housing allowances or Section 8 leasing of existing housing because these programs avoid building new units which is held to be inflationary.

In order to buttress the position, it is often stated that poor people's housing difficulties are caused not by the structures in which they live, but by their low-income. Spiro Agnew's last speech prior to his forced resignation was written by HUD aides and in it Agnew said housing is not a physical problem, but an income problem.

The Administration argued that what we really need is to move away from *supply* subsidies, *construction* subsidies, since they are too costly. They subsidize builders, not people who need the housing. Further, they concentrate the poor by building projects in specific areas. They do not give them a choice because they are told where they are going to live by designation of the projects at which poor people can live. They are not integrating people racially or economically because of the locations of these developments. Finally the programs are inequitable because they do not serve all the people they were intended to serve.

Behind all these criticisms is the Republican fear about the commitment the government is making, that is, the financial commitment. It goes back to the cost factor—that if all the people qualified for 236 and 235, and Rent Supplement—if they all just knocked on the door of the government and said look, this program is for us, we want it, then the government would have to calculate how many billions that would cost. That is what scared them—creating a rising expectation revolution. In order to put down the programs they said, "They cannot serve all the people they were meant to; therefore, they are inequitable."

So they come up with the housing allowance system which tries to meet all of these objections that they thought were inherent in the subsidy programs: 1) It subsidizes the person, the tenant, the resident, directly, putting the money directly in his pocket, not in the builder's pocket. 2) The person who has this housing allowance is

119

free to choose where he wants to live himself. The decision is not made by the builder or by the government; he is free to choose. 3) It is not an exorbitantly costly program because it does not in itself involve new construction; it makes maximum use of existing housing stock. That is a big issue—that we were not adequately utilizing the existing stock of housing.

HUD writers did not state these arguments for the first time—there had been scholarly work done in the last few years on the question of housing allowances. Housing allowances were first considered in the 1930's in the context of discussions about establishing the public housing program. The term used then was "rent certificates." President Eisenhower's Advisory Committee on Housing debated and rejected versions of the rent certificate idea in 1953. Then the Kaiser Committee in 1968, in reviewing the nation's housing policies, decided against housing allowances because of their concern about the inflationary impact on the housing market. The Kaiser Committee did receive strong recommendations for housing allowances in its staff research reports, and in a modest concession to its staff, the Committee suggested trying housing allowances on an experimental basis.

Based on the Kaiser Committee's recommendations, HUD contracted with the Urban Institute in Washington, D.C. to provide cost projections for a housing allowance system.

The Urban Institute concluded that allowances would cost in the range of $7.4 to $9.5 billion annually, based on assistance to 12.8 to 16.8 million Americans.

Simultaneously, Kansas City, Missouri and Wilmington, Delaware both funded small scale housing allowance experiments. The Kansas City experiment was administered by the Housing Development Information Center in Model Cities Neighborhoods and provided assistance to approximately 225 families.

Within this context, the Congress, upon passage of the Housing and Urban Development Act of 1970, directed HUD to establish an experimental housing allowance program to provide information on how families will use their allowances, how the market will respond, and how such allowances could be administered. Congress appropriated $10 million for Fiscal Years '72 and '73. HUD then contracted with the Urban Institute for the overall program design in March 1971. Subcontracts were made with Stanford Research Institute, ABT Associates, The Rand Corporation, and the MIT-Harvard Joint Center on Urban Studies. This experiment, authorized by Congress, was a result of preliminary study by the Urban Institute, which showed some promise of the concept.

So HUD's post-moratorium fixation on housing allowances comes after several years of academic and governmental exploration into the subject.

Arthur Solomon is one of the more cogent thinkers about housing allowances, and he and some other academicians had an impact on the planners at HUD. Solomon writes about the growing problems in the housing market and dissatisfaction with existing subsidy approaches.[1] He says policy makers have been faced with a choice of meeting the supply and demand strategies by pursuing a supply strategy to subsidize directly the construction or rehabilitation of dwellings for the poor, or assisting in the production of housing for higher income households, therefore hoping to set off a filter-down approach. The government would subsidize the actual rents paid by low income tenants and provide a general income maintenance or earmark income transfers for housing. In other words, in summary of these points, the federal government has the choice of subsidizing housing production or directly enhancing the effective demand for poor people.

Those who favor a demand- and consumer oriented strategy argue that cash transfers would be the most effective means of income redistribution. They maintain that a housing allowance would be less costly to the federal and local governments since there would be no tax shelters, developer profits, or increases in municipal services required.

Here are some of the goals that Solomon thinks are necessary to consider in making a judgment about whether housing allowances are more effective than production strategy: 1) Maximize aggregate housing consumption; in other words, which housing program contributes the most to the overall economic consumption. 2) Promote equal residential opportunities, or freedom of choice. 3) Close the housing gap in the most effective manner—the gap between ability to pay and need for housing. "In the most cost effective manner" means the least costly to the public. 4) Redistribute housing consumption equitably. This means help the people who need it most. Remember that HUD's argument was that the subsidy programs were not serving poor people. That was used as a count against them.

Now what Solomon and others have done is to take those goals and apply them to the subsidy programs, the production subsidy programs, and then estimate how the housing allowance approach would fare under their criteria.

The idea of maximizing consumption would work under a housing allowance system in those cases where what economists call an "elastic market" exists. If there is an "in-elastic market," then placing money in the hands of tenants during this tight market will drive up the cost of housing. Therefore, it would not achieve the goal of maximizing consumption. Solomon says that a perfectly in-elastic supply implies the need for government assisted construction programs, which directly increases the supply of housing to meet market demands. On the other hand, with a perfectly elastic supply, every additional dollar of housing expenditure results in the provision of an additional dollar of housing consumption. And this has always been the major issue in debates about housing allowances versus production, namely, that there are certain conditions which have to be met before it will work. There must be a relatively soft housing market, else in a tight housing market people will be exploited and dollars will be wasted.

Not too many places exist in the United States which are not subject to the impact of a tight market. The worst of course would be New York City. The same would be true in Boston. Among the the larger cities only Philadelphia would be a place where there is seemingly a large amount of housing that is empty where a good house could be subject to a small amount of repair.

What about "promoting equal residential cooportunity"?—that is, dispersing people, not concentrating them. The hope is that under ideal conditions putting the dollar into the pocket of individuals promotes consumer sovereignty. The person can choose the neighborhood, choose the type of house, choose the friends, and all that go with the free market system. The ideal seldom approaches reality. First, there is the racial discrimination. Second, exclusionary zoning "prevents many from exercising free choice." The desire of a person with cash in his pocket who would like to live in the house of his choice would be severely limited by the fact that in most cities of America zoning causes single family residential houses to be unrentable and determines the architectural and esthetic style of housing.

"Closing the housing gap," means doing the most amount of assisting for the least amount of money. It is often claimed that a 236 or Rent Supplement housing unit costs more to subsidize than an existing unit. For example, in Boston, Solomon showed that on a monthly basis, the government, in conventional public housing, had to pay $60 a month; in Rent Supplement new construction, $107 a month; rehabilitated Rent Supplement, $94; whereas in the leased public housing, the cost for existing units was $55 per month, which is the lowest of all those compared.

In the case of conventional public housing the Housing Authorities actually develop, administer, and operate the complex, whereas under the leased public housing program the same housing authority negotiates with landlords for the lease of private dwellings. Rent Supplement and 236 pass through the hands of FHA and local sponsors. The argument is that other parties are getting a part of the pie which poor people are not getting, and, therefore, the assumption is made that it costs $1600 per annum for a 236 unit— half of which really goes to investors, builders, and developers.

Solomon, after taking a look at these four goals and trying to analyze the subsidy approach, the supply approach, and the demand approach, came up with a conclusion that the existing production or income in-kind strategies are inappropriate. In other words, total reliance on one or the other is inappropriate.

> While such programs should be contingent, national housing policy should create a balance between production and consumer-oriented strategy. The latter approach—the consumer— which includes use of Public Housing in existing units, housing allowances, and income maintenance schemes is less costly, more equitable, and more responsive to the consumer choice. There is need for more emphasis on redistributive housing strategies which rely on direct cash transfer. But in order for these strategies to function optimally, it is necessary for all levels of Government to work toward the elimination of existing housing market barriers, such as racial discrimination, restrictive zoning, and collusive real estate practices, which impede full utilization of increments in rent paying ability.[2]

Have there ever been more conditional conditions? In other words, solve all the problems of society in America to which racial discrimination and restrictive zoning point, and then the income strategies will work.

To propose a housing assistance system which will work only if other, more fundamental, social problems are resolved, over an imperfect system which has at least provided opportunity for millions, must be cast in the light of misty idealism at best and cynical posturing at worst. In either case, the cause of better housing is not served.

Even if some credence is given to the housing allowance emphasis so popular in academic circles and at HUD, no straight thinking person would hold, based on the character of our housing needs, that *no* production should be a part of an overall housing strategy.

I have tried in Chapter I to evaluate the federally subsidized housing programs and why their demise was a fatal blow to the American economy and to the cause of decent housing.

When the moratorium was announced and during the period of national discussion about housing policy, I was, frankly, hesitant to say, simply reinstate the Rent Supplement, 236, and 235 programs, with the reforms outlined in the 1974 Senate bill. I say hesitant because I, like most citizens, had an inherent trust in the good sense of our public officials. I believed that the Administration was mistaken in imposing the moratorium, but I thought that the error would be corrected when the consequences became clear. Alas, the Haldeman entourage knew exactly the course it was following, and to me, as well as the Nation, the tenor of the Administration became clearer—HUD's casualties were a smaller battle in a larger war.

So it is not simple-minded to say American housing policy must return to the premises of the Housing Act of 1968, while responding to the "special challenge" of the 1970's.

A milestone of the Housing and Urban Development Act of 1968 was the articulation of a national housing goal. Congress, on the basis of the recommendations of HUD, the Kaiser Committee, and others set a target of producing 26 million units in ten years. At the time the figure was considered conservative, yet, as has often been the case in housing, even this modest goal will not be reached because of the pitifully low number of housing starts in the mid-1970's.

But the Nation must commit itself to a stated, achievable goal in order to fulfill the American people's housing needs. The next major housing act should begin on this note, and at least 2.5 to 3 million units annually are required.

In order to achieve this level of production the private sector must play the central role. The experience from 1969-72 with Section 235 and 236 showed that when private construction, financing, and management is combined with federal financial aid the goal can be achieved. It is not possible to "rely on the private market" unaided by some government assistance at the financing and construction stage, because too many Americans are priced out of that market.

The fuel of the American housing "engine" is capital from mortgage investors. A steady and productive housing industry requires a constant supply of mortgage funds on reasonable terms. Over the past decade the federal government has made great strides in stabilizing the flow of mortgage money by various fiscal devices, such as liberal use of the "Tandem Plan" whereby the Government National Mortgage Association (GNMA) purchases mortgages from the Federal National Mortgage Association (FNMA) at a price lower than the true cost, having the effect of bringing, say a 9 percent mortgage down to 7 ¾ percent. This device has assisted the middle-income housing market.

To assist the low and moderate income family to buy a home or rent an apartment, a government subsidy beyond the "Tandem Plan" is necessary, such as was the case in the 235 and 236 programs where the interest rate was subsidized down to 1 percent.

If the next housing act recommits the Nation to a production goal and is premised on the effective combination of private and public cooperation, what are the specific points needed to start the United States back on the road to recovery in the housing sector?

First, by a stroke of the pen the President could release approximately .5 billion dollars impounded in 1973. These funds, appropriated by Congress for the 235, 236, Rent Supplement and Public Housing programs could stimulate the construction of over three hundred thousand housing units for lower income Americans.

Second, the new housing act should reinstitute and then authorize new funds for the subsidy programs frozen since 1973. The revisions made by the Senate in its version of the 1974 Act would strengthen these programs and insure an even higher degree of success with them.

Third, HUD, as a U. S. Court decided, should immediately use appropriated funds to subsidize the operations of 236 projects subjected to extraordinary utility and property tax increases. This action would save many of the projects from foreclosure and further expense to the government, as well as keeping them from becoming more ammunition for the critics of the programs.

Fourth, a new housing act should contain a restructuring of the Section 8 program. The new revision should provide for federal assistance in the financing of housing to be leased under Section 8, as well as insuring that private lenders have the incentives to participate—such as guaranteed payment of rent.

Fifth, the adverse impact of Federal Reserve monetary policies must be blunted by strong Executive and Congressional action. The Federal Reserve usually deflects any suggestion of special treatment for housing and recommends legislative remedies as more appropriate. But, as was argued in the Introduction, federal monetary policies are so potent that fiscal measures by the government are not effective to counter them. The President should urge a less stringent money supply policy until the housing sector recovers. The President, together with the appropriate Congressional committees, should seriously consider a credit allocation program which would funnel credit to the hard-pressed housing industry while discouraging other lower priority capital expenditures.

A new housing effort in America cannot commence without a new era of cooperation between the private sector, the Administration, and Congress. It is often said that in foreign policy politics should stop at the water's edge. Housing is also too important to continually fall prey to the whims of political ideology and temper. We have a right to expect so basic a need as shelter to be met without the all too customary stops and starts caused by political theoreticians in HUD or OMB.

Several concrete steps must be taken to build this era of cooperation:

- HUD must be revitalized from top to bottom with a new sense of its original mission, to be the instrument by which the housing needs of America are fulfilled.

- The Administration and Congress must re-establish a working partnership, in a nonpartisan spirit. Mutual distrust has built up over the past few years because of HUD's disdain of Congressional prerogatives.

- HUD and the White House must seek more systematically the friendly cooperation of the private trade groups, so as to involve homebuilders, mortgage bankers, architects, housing officials, civil rights leaders, and others in the process of developing and implementing a new housing effort.

The Problem of HUD

The Department of Housing and Urban Development has been a consistent adversary of wider housing opportunity over the last three years. Persistently and at times arrogantly HUD has

- impounded millions of appropriated funds for Section 235 and 236, in the face of steady Congressional opposition, suspended the subsidy programs and refused to reinstate them even after Congressional authority was restated in 1974

126

- suspended the New Communities program, jeopardizing billions of dollars already invested in newly developed towns and millions spent in planning others,

- refused to use appropriated funds to subsidize operations of 236 projects beset by rising utility and tax costs, and

- delayed the implementation of the Section 8 program for *one year* after enactment of the law.

The primary reason for HUD's cavalier attitude toward Congress, the courts, and the American people is that the Haldeman-Ehrlichman tactic of "Nixonizing" the bureaucracy seems to have been most successfully attempted in that Executive Department.

A United States House of Representatives Subcommittee on Manpower has discovered that HUD kept political dossiers on more than four thousand employees and job applicants between 1969 and 1973. An article by the Los Angeles Times—Washington Post News Service, on June 18, 1975 reported that "Subcommittee investigators believe that the HUD operation represents the most serious political incursions into the federal merit system uncovered to date."

In Nixon's fist term all the high level, sub-cabinet positions were of course held by loyal Republicans. But after the 1972 election, Nixon asked for and received the resignation of every one of them (George Romney had already expressed his intention to resign). It was quite a spectacle. The Mormon FHA Commissioner, known for his hard-headed conservatism, appeared to me to be in a state of shock at the Home Builders Convention in Houston in January 1973. He was not so much shocked by the moratorium, as that he, a loyal Nixon supporter who had sacrificed his year as President of NAHB, would be given notice in the manner of a day laborer. And there was the black Assistant Secretary who had spent nearly all of 1972 garnering support for Nixon from black professionals. He, and many of them, believed that the Administration was sincere in its determination to make "black capitalism" a reality—even if it took some special HUD treatment, which was implied. How surprised was he, the highest ranking black official in the federal government, to get his pink slip along with the others.

In Romney's place, Haldeman engineered the appointment of James Lynn. Lynn had been a Cleveland corporate lawyer brought by the Administration to the Department of Commerce. At Commerce he was the Under Secretary, but his primary role was to be the White House (Haldeman) presence there.

127

Romney's resignation had been hoped for by the White House since 1969. Early on he clashed with the "Palace Guard," as Dan Rather called it. In his book by that name, he has some interesting words about Romney.[3] Romney offended Nixon at the very beginning of the Administration when he went in to the President in early 1969 and made a strong argument for the continuation of Model Cities. Nixon considered Model Cities "one of the worst boondoggles left over from Johnson's Great Society." Nixon had let it out through his aides that it was going to be discontinued, but Romney obtained a personal appointment with the President in an attempt to keep the program alive. The President agreed to relent. But, then immediately he said to Haldeman, "I wish that Romney had not pressed that on me—I didn't appreciate it." So from the beginning Romney was in bad grace with the President.

That also showed something about Nixon's character. Rather tries to illustrate, successfully, I think, that one reason why he had this "Palace Guard" is that Nixon was a coward—he could never have a personal confrontation. That is why he relied on Haldeman and why Haldeman said many times, "I am Nixon's SOB." He did not have the guts to say to Romney, "I don't want Model Cities." But that did not prevent him from saying "get Romney" because he pressed it on him.

So they had it in mind to fire him right off, but the famous Walter Hickel case came up. Hickel wrote a letter to the President expressing chagrin that Nixon was isolated from the youth, and did not seem to understand their feelings. Somehow someone in Hickel's office leaked this letter to the press about the same time the President got in. Haldeman called Hickel on the phone and said icily, "I have the letter Wally but it's already on the AP wire." Hickel did not get to talk to the President again until after he resigned. At the time of the letter they did not have the guts to fire him, they just let him hang on; they even cut him out of the White House religious services. He could not attend them.

When it was finally determined that they could let him go, John Mitchell was assigned to tell him to resign. Hickel said, "The only man who could ask me to quit would be the President." So they arranged a meeting with the President and Hickel. They did have a pleasant meeting, but the President said, "Wally, I think you had better go." When Hickel heard that, he resigned. By the time it took Hickel to get from the White House to the Interior Department, just a short drive, his office had been completely emptied and locked and six deputies had been fired by Haldeman and their offices emptied and locked.

Back to Romney. Because of Hickel they did not have the fortitude to fire Romney because of all the hoopla caused by the former Governor of Alaska. They could not fire another governor. Because of Hickel they did not fire Romney, but they started cutting him out also. He could not see the President. So, Romney performed the role of announcing the freeze and then Lynn was appointed.

And Haldeman had his man in charge of a department whose policies and programs needed an efficient beheading. Lynn was the one for the job, a "heel-clicker" in the words of a former Commerce Secretary. He had no previous experience in housing. But what experience was required to impound, to freeze, to withhold, in short, to preside over the demise of the Department's programs and to do it in opposition to Congress and the public? The job called for a public relations flim-flam, which is exactly what Lynn delivered—via the infamous *Housing in the Seventies* and, what is now clear, a flurry of talk about housing allowances and Section 8, but no concrete, positive action. As the powerful Director of the Office of Management and Budget, Lynn continued in 1976 to cast his macabre spell over HUD, by unilaterally reducing HUD's allocation of funds for Section 8.

Why would Haldeman have the audacity, however, to pull off the Lynn appointment in the face of strong housing lobby opposition and in total disregard of Congressional leaders? Part of the reason lies in the vulnerability of HUD to such a White House assault.

HUD is the second youngest of our Cabinet-level Departments. When it was created in 1965, the FHA and the Public Housing Administration, especially, considered themselves rather independent and responsible to their own constituencies. To counter this required an executive leader with strong White House support. The first secretary, Robert C. Weaver, was not a firm administrator, nor did President Johnson give him sustained support. Indeed, the President had undermined Weaver by making him wait several months after creation of the Department to appoint him as Secretary.

Romney was an excellent leader, and during the first Nixon term accomplished more in housing production than really could have been achieved by any lesser man with the White House burdens he bore.

But, it is clear that HUD's internal history is a major problem and caused a fatal weakness laying it open to a Haldeman *putsch*. Other federal departments and agencies felt the strong hand of Haldeman. The method was common—put a loyalist in, at the top or at least near the top—and then exercise control of policy from the White House. If many other departments or agencies had been as weak as HUD, the Nixonizing of the federal government would probably have been more obvious to the American people. Then we would not have had to wait until the Watergate revelations to demonstrate how the Nixon Administration intended to destroy independent centers of power which would not conform to its wishes.

Unfortunately, the Ford Administration has continued to keep HUD in its ironic role of adversary of housing. In a politically astute move Ford nominated a woman, Carla Hills, to be Lynn's successor. Congressmen, who again were exasperated to have a HUD Secretary with no housing experience, could hardly oppose a female appointment to the Cabinet.

Mrs. Hills has not changed the course of HUD. The same assistants and speech writers from the Lynn days are advising the new Secretary. In a typical statement, she made clear she does not regard Section 8 as a housing production vehicle at all, but rather "a program to help poor people."[4] The meaning of this is that she, like Lynn, would really like to see Section 8 as a substitute housing allowance program that goes to poor residents of *existing* housing. Anything that smacks of a 236-like production vehicle is suspect.

More seriously, HUD continues to flout Congressional intent and even Court decisions. For instance, in May 1975 the U. S. District Court for Maryland, commenting on HUD's refusal to provide operating subsidies to 236 projects as authorized by Section 212 of the 1974 Housing Act, said:

> Simply put HUD has adopted the position that it will not implement the program in any way. Claiming that it has been given broad discretion by Congress to make these payments, HUD has decided that it will exercise such discretion to make no payments at all to any projects at any time, whether worthy or not and whether the project might fully qualify under the Congressional standards or not.

> The reason for HUD's approach are quite frankly stated in the Secretary's brief and are further stated in argument. HUD purely and simply disagrees with the congressional policy.[5]

The Court went on to declare that it is not HUD's prerogative to disagree with congressional policy and refuse to implement it.

But, unfortunately, this is the position too often taken by HUD in the last few years.

Another federal district court in Connecticut found the same attitude displayed by HUD in respect to the relation between Community Development funds and housing. HUD took the position that suburban towns around Hartford could apply for grants for Community Development without including estimates of the housing needs of low income persons "expected to reside in the community." But the Court ruled HUD did not have the power to waive compliance with the requirements of the Housing and Community Development Act of 1974. The Judge said,

> If the statute gave specific directions, or the Administration interpretation is not consistent with either the statutes or the Congressional intent, the Administrative agency cannot amend it by regulation.[6]

Both courts' decisions illustrate the rather blatant disregard for law on the part of HUD.

As Shakespeare might say, it is "bootless" to think that there can be any resurgence of interest and support for decent housing for all until the very federal agency responsible for achieving this goal is revitalized and changed throughout. The day when the highest housing officials begin to *advocate* rather than *attack* housing programs will be the day the Nation at least has a fair shot at the target.

HUD has been demoralized by the illegal and arrogant actions of its leaders, and even if Congress finally prevails in reinstating the subsidy programs, the new Secretary will have to be a committed and persuasive spokesman who can rebuild what has been cruelly and criminally destroyed. I hope he or she is waiting and preparing for that new day.

Conclusion: A New Value

Houston, like every city, proclaims its values by the physical structures which form its skyline, its cityscape. To any visitor the downtown plethora of sharp, geometric blocks which house Exxon, Shell, Tenneco, and Pennzoil are impressve symbols of an opulent, petroleum-based metropolis which knows no recession.

The newest addition to Houston's sparkling complex of multi-storied wonders is the twin towered Pennzoil Building. The oil company's headquarters is an architectural tour de force, with its slanted tops forming a wedge in the sky. It was designed by Phillip Johnson.

Confronted each day by the visual impact of Johnson's building

131

rising higher and higher on Houston's scene, and of course working each day in the effort to improve housing, I was pleasantly startled to read an interview by Lee Radziwill with him in *Esquire Magazine*, December 1974. The creator of the new skyscraper said,

> If I put the same energy in (a) housing complex that I put in on the headquarters of an oil company, the results would be similar. It would be used for a different purpose and *someday somebody is going to insist on the quality of housing being at least the quality of a commercial skyscraper or better.* Just because it hasn't been is the fault of our society and the stupid way we've handled housing. (Emphasis added)

Johnson's insight about housing's equal importance with sky-scrapers leads him to a fascinating prediction:

> If government housing is going to constitute the tasks for the next decade—and that's what I believe—I would be delighted to do that as I would the skyscrapers I am doing now. . .

Lee Radziwill, his interlocutor, vacuously reveals a too typical attitude in America in her response to Johnson's words:

> I don't know why you say that, because it has so many limitations on it. That it's very depressing.

Johnson's view of housing as the task for the next decade is bold and perceptive. It takes the measure of our skewed emphasis on ostentatious commercialism to the detriment of decent housing for all Americans. When our society values the family environment as well as the business environment, then we will not only have Penn-zoil buildings, but also homes to which he, not modestly of course, and others will devote as much creative force and technical skill.

The first step in the recognition of such a value will be the federal government's firm commitment to the policy of a decent home for every American family. As Johnson said, "We could spend the same amount of money on people's houses . . . as we do on skyscrapers. Why Not?"

Indeed, Why Not?

For this is a task which can be *accomplished*—the private builder is capable, the private mortgage industry is capable, but the support of the federal government is necessary. And if we can be first in space, first in military defense, first in international commerce, we can also be first in housing.

America faces the challenge of a revolution in the housing market and for too many life in our cities is marred by men and women huddled in crowded slums, in neighborhoods which need to be revived. Why not spend our treasure and energy in the effort to build a slumless America?

Long ago, the philosopher Maimonides asserted that the "foremost giver" is he who assists the poor man to become self-supporting. Helping a man obtain a deed to his own home or rent a decent place to live is surely one way to overcome the ironic gap between the nation's ability to provide housing and the incapacity to afford that housing by so many. We must bring the lower-income family into full participation in a prosperous America, and a fundamental requirement is a decent home for all.

END NOTES

PREFACE
1. Boston *Globe*, August, 1975.

CHAPTER I
1. U.S., President's Committee on Urban Housing, *A Decent Home*. National Commission on Urban Problems, *Building the American City* (Washington, D.C.: U.S. Government Printing Office, 1968).
2. President Nixon's Message on Housing, September 19, 1973.
3. Anthony Downs, *Federal Housing Subsidies: Their Nature and Effectiveness and What We Should Do About Them*, Summary Report, October, 1972, p. 25.
4. Congressional Research Service, Library of Congress, Critique of "Housing in the Seventies." Prepared in Response to a Request by the Housing and Urban Affairs Subcommittee of the Senate Committee on Banking, Housing and Urban Affairs. (Washington, D.C.: U.S. Government Printing Office, 1974).
5. Ibid.
6. Ibid.
7. Ibid.
8. "Errors in program management were responsible for most of the failures in (the) subsidized . . . housing programs." "Housing Subsidies and Housing Policy," Report of Joint Economic Committee, March 5, 1973.
9. Anthony Downs, op. cit., at p. 25.
10. Edmund Burke, *Reflections on the French Revolution* (New York: Bobbs-Merrill, 1955), p. 70.
11. Ibid., at pp. 89, 109-110.
12. Ibid., at p. 197.
13. Ibid., at p. 198.
14. Ibid., at p. 199.

CHAPTER II
1. Ada Louise Huxtable, *Will They Ever Finish Bruckner Boulevard?* (New York: Macmillan, 1971), pp. 167-171.

CHAPTER III
1. Herbert Gans, *Urban Villagers* (New York: Glencoe, 1962).
2. Martin Anderson, *The Federal Bulldozer* (Cambridge: MIT Press, 1964).
3. Berman v. Parker, 348 U.S. 26 (1954), established the principle that the Urban Renewal program was a proper exercise of constitutional authority, since the condemnation of private property for redevelopment was adjudged to be a public purpose.
4. Claude Brown, *Manchild in the Promised Land* (New York: Macmillan, 1965), pp. 5-6.
5. Marc Fried and Peggy Gleicher, "Some Sources of Residential Satisfaction in an Urban Slum," *Journal of the American Institute of Planners* 27, No. 4, (November, 1961): 305.
6. Cf. William Lee Miller, *The Fifteenth Ward and the Great Society* (Boston: Houghton Mifflin, 1966), p. xv.

CHAPTER IV
1. Since 1968, Congress has delegated the authority to set the FHA rate to the Secretary of Housing and Urban Development.

135

2. Charles Haar, *Federal Credit and Private Housing* (New York: McGraw-Hill, 1960), p. 56.

CHAPTER V

1. Blake McKelvey, *The Urbanization of America: 1860-1915* (New Brunswick, N.J.: Rutgers University Press, 1963), p. 80.

2. Ibid.

3. U.S., National Commission on Urban Problems, *Legal Remedies for Housing Code Violations*, Frank P. Grad. Research Report No. 14, 1968, p. 62.

4. See, for example. Health Department v. Rector of Trinity Church, 145 N.Y. 32, 39 N.E. 833 (1895): Tenement House Department v. Moeschen, 179 N.Y. 325, 72 N.E. 231 (1904). Aff'd *per curiam*, 203 U.S. 583 (1906): Queenside Hills Realty Co., v. Wilson, 294 N.Y. 917, 63 N.E. 2d 116 (1945), Aff'd *sub nom*. Queenside Hills Realty Co. v. Sail, 328 S.W. 80 (1946).

5. Cf., Frank P. Grad, op. cit., chapter XII.

6. Frank v. Maryland, 359 U.S. 360 (1959); Camara v. Municipal Court, 387 U.S. 523 (1967); See v. City of Seattle, 387 U.S. 541 (1967).

7. The nation's new housing construction each year accounts for less than 3 percent of the total supply. Yet a fourth of all housing units are deteriorating, dilapidated, or lack a sanitary facility. Thus, "new building alone will not provide suitable housing for all or most of our poor families." Alvin L. Schorr, *Explorations in Social Policy* (New York: Basic Books, 1968), p. 195.

8. U.S., National Commission on Urban Problems, Report of the Commission, *Building the American City* (Washington, D.C.: U.S. Government Printing Office, 1968), p. 277.

9. M. Carter McFarland, ed., *Residential Rehabilitation* (Minneapolis: University of Minnesota, 1965), p. 3.

10. Schorr, op. cit., p. 198.

11. Cf. U.S., National Commission on Urban Problems, *Importance of the Property Tax*, Dick Netzer. Research Report No. 1, 1968.

12. Cf. U.S., National Commission on Urban Problems, *The Federal Income Tax in Relation to Housing*, Richard E. Slitor. Research Report, No. 5, 1968.

13. Schuyler Jackson, "Housing Code Inspection Subjected to Some Critical Comments and Some Suggestions for the Future." *Journal of Housing* Vol. 27 (October, 1970): 530-533.

14. Schorr, op. cit., p. 198.

15. The model codes are the American Public Health Association Code, the Southern Standard Code, and those of the International Conference of Building Officials and the Building Officials Conference of America.

16. National Housing and Development Law Project, *Handbook on Housing Law* (Berkeley and Los Angeles: University of California, 1970), Chapter III, Part II, p. 4.

CHAPTER VII

1. Bulletin of the National Housing and Economic Law Project at Berkeley, California, Vol. 2, Issue 10, (November 15, 1972).

CHAPTER VIII

1. Reynolds v. Sims, 377 U.S. 533 (1964).

CHAPTER X

1. Arthur Solomon, "Housing and Public Policy Analysis," in *Housing Urban America*, Pynoos, Schafer, and Hartman, eds., (Chicago: Aldine Publishing, 1973). See also Solomon's *Housing the Urban Poor* (Cambridge: MIT Press, 1974).

2. Ibid., p. 576.

3. Dan Rather, *The Palace Guard* (New York: Harper and Row, 1975).

4. *Housing and Development Reporter*, p. 1232.

5. Ross v. Community Services, May 16, 1975. Quoted from *Housing and Development Reporter* Vol. 3, No. 1 (June 2, 1975): 5-6.

6. City of Hartford, et al. v. Hills, et al., (DC, District of Connecticut) Civil No. H-75-258, 1-28-76, pp. 13, 742.